CONSCIENCE *Versus* LAW

CONSCIENCE
Versus
LAW

*reflections on the evolution of
natural law*

BY

MONSIGNOR JEREMIAH NEWMAN, M.A., PH.D.
President, St. Patrick's College,
Maynooth, Co. Kildare.

FRANCISCAN HERALD PRESS
1434 WEST 51st STREET • CHICAGO, 60609

CONSCIENCE VERSUS LAW
COPYRIGHT
©1971 JEREMIAH NEWMAN
FIRST PUBLISHED 1971 BY
THE TALBOT PRESS
89 TALBOT STREET, DUBLIN 1
AND IN THE UNITED STATES OF AMERICA BY
FRANCISCAN HERALD PRESS
1434 WEST 51ST STREET, CHICAGO 60609

Nihil obstat: Jacobus Ambrose
Imprimi potest: ✠ Henricus
          Episcopus Limericensis
          die 4a Maii 1971

Library of Congress Catalog Card No. 70–175146
ISBN 8199–0437–6

Printed in the Republic of Ireland by the Book Printing Division
of Smurfit Print and Packaging Ltd., Dublin 9.

TO
THE STUDENTS OF MAYNOOTH 1970-71

Contents

Preface

The greater portion of this book has resulted from a series of lectures delivered in the School of Theology of the University of San Francisco and my own observations. Developments of papers read to the National University of Ireland Graduates Club, London, and the Christus Rex Society Congress, make up the latter part of the book.

I would like to take this opportunity to thank some friends, whose hospitality and patience made the writing of the book possible. I refer in particular to Harold and Mary Anne Berliner of Grass Valley, California, with whom I spent some wonderful working week-ends, and Carol and Ed. Blake of New York, with the help of whose company on Nantucket Island the manuscript was virtually completed.

I trust that this book, modest though it is, may prove to be of some value in the rehabilitation of natural law.

JEREMIAH NEWMAN

Maynooth,
March, 1971

Introduction

HISTORIANS OF the future writing about our age will most probably describe it as "The Age of Liberty". A preoccupation with freedom is one of the most notable characteristics of contemporary secular and religious society.

In the secular sphere the catch-cry is "civil rights", in the pursuit of which riots and revolutions have become almost a normal feature of everyday life in most countries. Youth, in particular, is on the warpath, as witness the events in so very many universities in which the students —and oftentimes also the staff—are seeking a major role in the determination of their own affairs. The upshot of it all is that authority and law, as these have existed, are under heavy pressure and undergoing considerable change. Indeed the extreme wing of current dissent, believing reform of society impossible, have opted to drop out of it altogether. For these, such as the members of the extra-establishment communes that are springing up in America, the choice is for a non-institutional, community way of life that in theory at least would seem to be close to anarchy.

In the religious sphere a somewhat analogous situation has developed. One continually hears about the "rights of conscience", in the pursuit of which protest and rebellion have become almost a normal feature of everyday life in the Church. Here again one discerns a definite seeking by the younger generation for a substantial say in the fashioning of their life-styles. In the academic sphere the emphasis is on freedom of decision, particularly as regards the content of moral teaching. Again the upshot of it all is that authority and law in the Church also are currently experiencing difficulty and strain. And, as in the case of secular society, there is emerging an extreme wing of dissent, which despairs of reforming the Church along the lines desired and which opts instead to drop out of the establishment. For these, such as the members of what is called the underground Church in America, the choice is for a non-institutional community way of life which in its own way approaches closely to anarchy.

Both in society and Church in fact the situation is such that a choice between authority and anarchy seems to be pending. In face of this it behoves thinking people to investigate as best they can how due order with due freedom can best be ensured, how authority in both society and Church can be preserved, while allowing proper scope to the liberty of the individual.

There is one sphere and, to my mind, one sphere only in which this problem common to both orders can be discussed. I refer to the sphere of what is known as the natural law, in which society and the Church have traditionally found a mutual meeting place. It will be the thesis of this book that natural law, as understood against the entire background of its history, provides the elements of a solution to the problem, that it supplies a legal framework within which authority in secular society must perforce respect the rights of the individual, that it also supplies a moral framework within which authority in the Church must equally respect the rights of the individual conscience—while in both cases, preserving this authority intact and avoiding deterioration into anarchy.

It will be one of the main features of the book to describe how a decline in natural law thinking has been responsible for the appearance of tendencies towards absolutism and, by way of reaction to this, of legal and moral arbitrariness. This is demonstrably the case in the sphere of legality, where abandonment of natural law for the will of the legislator has led slowly but surely to juridical arbitrariness. In the sphere of morality the deterioration of natural law theory has yet not gone so far as to make a hindsight available to us. A hindsight which would show that the replacement of law by individual decision unavoidably leads to a kind of conscientious licence. But if an argument from analogy has any force at all, what has happened in the legal sphere should put us on our guard in the moral.

A renewed emphasis on natural law, in its fullest dimensions, could provide the key that is needed to the present discontent. This calls for a historical approach to the elucidation of the matter, for natural law has become quite deformed over the course of the centuries. Whereas for many—both secular and religious—it has come to be understood as a rigid body of inflexible precepts, which leave no room for differences stemming from individual or social circumstances, natural law will prove to be a remarkably flexible thing, capable of progress, of development, of historicity, as human culture varies and develops. It will emerge too that this historicity of natural law has a religious dimension deriving from the fact of Jesus Christ. Nature is not destroyed by the supernatural and just as, in the secular sphere, what is of natural law can be somewhat different from culture to culture, in the context of Christian culture it can also be different.

An important aspect of natural law theory throughout its history until relatively recently, has been the role assigned to the community in determining its content. This is most notable in ancient times but was also a feature of the medieval period. There is great need for a return to this perspective today, both in secular society and the Church. In the former the philosophy of democracy, if it could only be got to work really well, contains the necessary elements that are required to defend freedom. In the latter the new theology of the Church as community could perform a similar function and yield similar results. A legal and moral teaching deriving from a natural law theory and appreciative of the role of the community, would go a long way towards meeting what is wanted. It would allow due liberty to the individual while endowing authority in both spheres with the moral backing that is necessary if it is to be effective.

But it will also emerge that unless one holds on to a concept of natural law as something "given", there is no escaping a legal and moral relativity. That the community and through it the individual, has a role to play must not be doubted, but it must never be interpreted as being constitutive of either legality or morality. Nor should the function of authority be conceived as consisting in the mere formulation of law or morals as the tendencies of the community dictate. There is no room at all for such views in the longer tradition of natural law. Neither legality nor morality are fundamentally subjective. They are objective realities to be discovered rather than agreed upon, discovered in the context of community under the guidance and direction of authority. It is a two-way process, in which the community is subject to authority but in which authority does not ignore the views of the community. To forget the latter would lead straight to absolutism; to forget the former would lead equally directly to anarchy.

1

The Ancients' Search for Justice

THE ANCIENT world scarcely spoke at all of "natural law". What discussion there was among the ancients, and which later came to be known as natural law morality, was usually in terms of a quest for "justice".

Justice for the ancients was of two kinds—a dichotomy which goes back to the very earliest times. On the one hand there was justice in the sense of a "tit for tat", a something which centred on the idea of restoring equality, a virtue which the Pythagoreans identified with the square number four and which was later defined by Ulpian and the Roman jurists as "that which gives to each man his due". It was this virtue which the early Christian Fathers later classified with prudence, temperance and fortitude as a "cardinal" virtue.

Side by side with this there has always been a quite different idea of justice, meaning "righteousness" or the possession of all the virtues. It is in this sense that Joseph is described in the Bible as a just man and the same concept is to be found in ancient secular literature. The big difference between the biblical and the secular concepts is that whereas the former envisaged justice as something attainable only in a theological context—through obedience to divinely revealed law—for the latter, it was realizable in the socio-political context—though obedience to the law of the State.

At the present day, when morals have become so much a matter for the individual alone, it is not easy to understand this linking of virtue (justice) with the domain of politics. An insight into the intellectual background to this is essential to any grasp of the ancients' approach to natural morality.

For the ancient world individual and political morality were very much one and the same thing. What I mean is that one could succeed in being a good man only if one succeeded in being a good citizen. The search for the one was also a search for the other.

These perspectives were largely the product of the kind of State that existed at the time, the Greek *polis* or city state, small in size and easily governed, with an intimate atmosphere which permitted its rulers to interest themselves in every aspect of the life of its citizens. It was a Church and a school as much as a State. To be exiled from it was to lose all one valued—one's university and one's Gods as much as one's livelihood. It is for this reason that Plato's *Republic*, which set out to treat of life in such a State, has been acclaimed as a textbook—indeed the first textbook—of Ethics and Education as much as it is a textbook of Politics. One became a good man—one was moral and just—by being a good citizen within the system of justice which the State prescribed.

There is an immediate contrast between this and the later ethic of Christianity, according to which to be a good man was to strive to be like Christ. In this latter perspective morality was conceived as personal con-

6

formation to a model. The more ancient pagan world
thought differently. It is true that Plato looked upon
Socrates as a model, "a man whom I should not hesitate
to call the most righteous man then living", one who
might indeed be held up to others to imitate. But he
thought that such imitation was possible only to the few.
For the majority of men the essential precondition of
virtue was the socio-political framework of the State in
which they lived. Unless justice could be enshrined in
society, by and large it was not possible for the individual.

Classical scholars tell us that Plato's preoccupation
with ensuring the creation of a just society derived in no
small part from his disillusionment with the Athens which
had been responsible for the death of his hero Socrates,
thereby manifesting the failure of Greek civic life to construct a political framework which would train people to
live properly. In this his search for the blueprint of a
just society resembles somewhat the contemporary search
on the part of certain German writers for reliable principles of political morality following their experience of
the genocide of the Jews during the Hitler era. Be this as
it may, for the ancient world in general, morality or
justice was something attainable only within political
society.

The basic question for the ancient world—in Ethics
as well as in Politics—was "How is justice realized in
society?" And to this everybody answered: By respect
for "nomos", which inculcates right conduct in the community. By "nomos" was understood whatever determined
conduct, whether one calls it custom, mores or law. Hence
the immediate emergence of a further question: "What
exactly is meant by law?"

Plato's contribution to answering this is of supreme
importance. He was not, it is true, a professional jurist,
but his was the earliest important contribution to legal
philosophy. Before him notions about law were frag-

mentary—some lines of poetry from people like Pindar, some sayings of Solon, and some scrappy ideas attributed to the group called the Sophists. Yet such as they were, Plato learned from them all. He warmly embraced the sentiments of Pindar and Solon and vigorously rejected those of the Sophists.

For Solon the fundamental idea was that the happiness of the State—and therefore of the individual citizen—depends on the observance of sound laws. Beyond this, however, he did not go. Pindar on the other hand did, emphasizing the idea that law is, as he put it, the "Lord of all"—*nomos basileus panton*—something which *imposes itself* by its inherent rightness. Here we have one of the earliest expressions of the notion of "intrinsicality", the idea that something can stem from an order that is above man and, as a result, is unchangeable and the same for all. It was in this fashion that Pindar conceived of law as pertaining to the social dimension of *phusis* or nature. Just as in the physical domain nature imposes its demands with ineluctable necessity, so also in the domain of human conduct, freely chosen though it may be, there is a due order to be observed which stems from nature and which it is not within the power of man to interfere with.

Right contrary to these ideas were those of the Sophists, the logical analysts of the ancient world. For these, law was a relative and subjective thing that could differ from place to place and time to time. This was something which flowed inevitably from the relativism and subjectivism that were a distinctive feature of general Sophist thought. Perhaps the best-known expression in a nutshell of what the Sophists stood for was Protagoras's statement that "Man is the measure of all things". Here you had a relativism that would deny all absolute truths and a subjectivism that would proclaim that there are only human opinions.

All of which was reflected in the legal notions of Callicles, to the effect that law is "the opinion of the many"; in other words, what the majority stand for. Thus, as the Sophists saw things, while *nomos*—law—still projected the aspect of "imposition", it was no longer something which imposes itself by reason of its intrinsic rightness, but rather something which is imposed by decision. It was essentially the product of man rather than of nature; it came from man rather than to him.

It was only a step from this to the well-known doctrine of a third Sophist, Thrasymachus, that justice and law represent "the interest of the stronger". This, of course, is only to be expected if law is really the opinion of the many. For the many—the majority—are usually the stronger and can succeed in imposing their opinions on others. There is a salutary reminder here of the fact that the notion of the sovereignty of the people, as propounded by the theorists of modern democracy, can easily lead to what has been called "totalitarian democracy". To believe that the views of the majority must necessarily be just is nothing else than to follow Thrasymachus.

At any rate, for the Sophists, law was understood as entirely the invention of man, something arbitrarily decided upon and relating therefore to convention rather than to nature. Justice and morality followed suit.

There is one aspect of these Sophist views on law and morality which showed a hard-headedness that Plato did not always have. I refer to the empirical bent of all their thought. Indeed there is a certain resemblance between what they had to say and those modern theories concerning the essentially sociological character of law and morality. Law is what in fact is obeyed by people; morality what is regarded as right and wrong. As we shall see later, there is a place for empiricism. To conceive of law and morality from a purely rationalist basis is to risk ending up in unrealism. For a law that ignores facts is utterly useless, however right it may seem to be conceptually. It was in its lack of appreciation for the fact that the American people were simply not prepared to accept it that the prohibition law became a dead letter overnight. Church law too is not innocent of examples of prescriptions which take insufficient account of facts. The fasting regulations of the past, which imposed an equally rigorous diet during the Lenten season on the faithful all over the world, was nothing if not forgetful of the fact that there is a world of difference between Northern and Southern climes. No wonder a German moralist of the eighteenth century should have penned bitter lines to Rome on the subject: "Send us your blue skies, your bursting figs, your hanging grapes and we will fast with you".

In the same way, moral prescriptions that are insufficiently attentive to fact, especially by ignoring what people are unable to do, or are not prepared to do, can be unrealistic to the point of even being invalid. We shall have a lot to say about this again later. It will suffice here to point out that Plato, by an over-rejection of the views of the Sophists, by tending to see law from an exclusively rationalist or conceptualist standpoint, for a time at least forgot the importance of the empirical side of things and did not entirely escape the pitfall of unrealism.

Not that Plato himself was unaware of this. As a matter of fact, in his later years, he tried to correct it. But he was more concerned with avoiding the relativism and subjectivism which a purely empirical approach to law and morality involve. In this he exemplifies a perennial problem which once again faces us today. In the domain of natural law morality, in particular, we are once more confronted—especially over the birth control issue —with the age-old choice: whether to attempt a solution by way of an abstract consideration of the factors involved or whether to take one's cue from the concrete reactions of men in general?

The problem, as we shall see, is not new. It goes right back to the origins of the Western intellectual tradition, as evidenced by the debate between the Sophists and Plato.

This debate is best exemplified by the dialogue known as the *Minos* which, although its authenticity is disputed, is accepted as containing genuinely Platonic thought. If it is not from Plato's own hand, it at least reflects his sentiments as a painting from the school of Rembrandt does the style of the master. In it Plato—as always through the mouth of Socrates—conducts a discussion which teases out the subject gradually but surely and bit by bit arrives at conclusions.

Socrates opens by posing the question: "What is law?" His companion replies: "What kind of laws do you mean?" To which Socrates answers in the form of a further question: "Is there any difference between law and law as law?" The companion volunteers the view that law is that which is accepted as legal, at once indicating his allegiance to the Sophists. And so Socrates pounces at once. Law, he says, cannot be just what is accepted as legal, no more than speech is the thing that is spoken or vision that which is seen. His companion therefore attempts a clarification. Law consists of the decrees of the community, i.e. the opinion of the State. But Socrates will have none of this. He lets fly with all he has. Law in itself is always a good thing, but public decrees, as everyone knows, can be evil. Hence it is that if law consists of the decrees of the community, there can be question of the good decrees only. Or to put it differently, if law is the opinion of the State, it is good opinion, that is, true opinion that is in question. In other words, law is the discovery of reality with respect to the administration of the State. Here in his turn the Platonic Socrates is giving vent to the notion of intrinsicality in respect of law.

His companion then comes up with the bogey of the relativists. Surely law cannot be something absolute because the laws of different countries differ. Socrates has his answer ready: true though this is, no society—not even that of the Persians (which was regarded as properly barbaric)—believes that what is just for one country can be unjust for another, under the same respect and given the same circumstances. In these conditions, in so far as there are differences, they are attributed by all to ignorance.

And so the dialogue ends. As outlined in it, for Plato—through the mouth of Socrates—law is conceived as the discovery of reality, of truth in the sphere of political administration. It is the expression of how society should be organized so as to truly serve the interests of the citizens. In no way is it the fruit of arbitrary decision but rather of an accurate perception of how things are.

As in the case of the Sophists, so also Plato's notion of law was linked with his general philosophy. It is easy to see why this is so. If, as was maintained by Plato, genuine (i.e. reliable) knowledge consists in a body of abstract truths (or "ideas" as he called them) that are of a different order from the mass of concrete sense data which continually flow in upon us, then it behoves us to establish laws on the basis of conceptual appreciation rather than on the fleeting knowledge that accompanies sense experience. Concrete experience is shadow rather than substance; it produces opinions rather than a grasp of reality. This latter entails a deeper approach by way of conceptual formation, whereby abstract ideas are arrived at. Thus it is that, in the realm of aesthetics, reliable knowledge, truth, the discovery of reality, is attained, not just by way of the concrete experience of knowing beautiful things but by a rational appreciation of the abstract idea of beauty. It is exactly the same in the case of justice.

This body of abstract ideas, which constituted real knowledge for Plato, has at times been compared to the truths of revelation as understood by Christian theology, at other times to the truths of mathematics as given by science. But there are important differences between the one and the other. First of all, unlike the truths of revelation, the Platonic ideas do not at all derive from God. They are entirely the product of the intellect of man, of human reason. In fact, it is highly debatable whether Plato, or Aristotle after him, believed at all in the existence of a deity. What references to the gods are to be found in their works may well have been but a gesture to the beliefs of their day. Plato never forgot the fate of the agnostic Socrates, who had been sentenced on a charge of corrupting the youth. And both he and Aristotle wished to "sell" their books and to avoid alienating the populace and the censor. For these reasons their theological asides are suspect. Plato certainly believed that truth was attainable by a rationalist process of human intellection. It may be an exaggeration to interpret him as positing the existence of a world of ideas in which abstract concepts had a sort of independent existence, according to the view that is generally known as extreme realism. But he did hold that the only really valid knowledge of reality consisted in a kind of rational intuition of abstract concepts. An intuition which had nothing to do with the deity. In later times, Christian Neo-Platonists were to seek to baptize this by linking it with a form of mysticism or prayer. An even more direct effort to Christianize it by attributing the origin of the ideas to God took the form known as the theory of divine illumination. In one way or another, this Christian Platonism is to be found in St. Augustine, in Malebranche and in Berkeley.

Despite the *Timaeus,* it would be a mistake to think that Plato himself knew anything of such theology. Neither is it exactly accurate to compare the Platonic ideas with the truths of mathematics. For unlike the latter, the former are not empirically verifiable but are known only to a small minority of philosophers. The ancient world did not believe in human equality; slaves indeed were not regarded as men at all. It was Cicero who classified tools under three distinct headings—vocal, semi-vocal and mute. The mute category covered items like hammers or knives; the semi-vocal, oxen and other domestic animals, while by vocal tools he meant the class of slaves. Even those who were certainly human were regarded as differing *inter se* to such an extent that not all could attain to knowledge, the only knowledge, that is, which counts—the rational knowledge of abstract concepts.

Hence it was that the knowledge of justice, which was an essential requirement for morality, was a commodity capable of being acquired of themselves only by a minority, an intellectual aristocratic *élite*. To these alone was given the necessary rational insight. As rulers—for they should be rulers—they would seek to incarnate their vision in such a way that others could attain to justice.

It is interesting to note that Plato, like Socrates before him, seemed to believe that to know justice would also be to practise it. Knowledge and virtue were one. The philosopher-ruler would discover it and follow it for himself; through him it was open to others to have its implications placed before them. Once presented with what is just they would follow it. Force would be entirely unnecessary for securing moral conduct on the part of the individual.

For a while, during the period in which he wrote *The Republic*, Plato thought that even law would not be necessary. At least not law as commonly understood. Justice, it is true, must always stem from *nomos*. But *nomos* he conceived as the fruit of the art of the philosopher-ruler, whose adaptable intelligence took account of individual circumstances. It was much more a body of *ad hoc*—but by no means arbitrary—directives than a rule of law as this is generally understood. The ruler would guide his citizens to achieve justice in all their doings by a kind of omnipresent and omni-competent charismatic wisdom.

In his later works, *The Statesman* and *The Laws,* Plato came to realize that such benevolent dictatorship is an entirely impossible ideal. This change of view is partly to be explained by his own bitter experience when asked to introduce the system of *The Republic* into Syracuse. The complete failure of his attempt brought him down to earth. Hence it was that, in his later works, Plato came to insist that it is essential to have a rule of law. He continued to maintain that this remained a second best arrangement when compared to the ideal of *The Republic.* But second best or not, it was more realistic. It is impossible to develop a practical system whereby all the concrete decisions of the citizens can be guided by the ruler. The best that can be done in the conditions of the real world is for him to frame laws that will cover the generality of problems.

Under a rule of law as thus conceived there will always be hard cases, where the law will fail to take due account of individual circumstances. For law is geared to meet the needs of the "average" man—an entity which has no concrete existence. Nevertheless, this is as much as can be achieved.

Here we have what might be called the Platonic dilemma. On the one hand, a rule of law is necessary if the unrealism of the charismatic and unstructured society is in any way to be successfully avoided. On the other hand, under law there is another unrealism, that of legislating for an entity which has no concrete existence, and therefore inevitably courting the danger of being irrelevant to the situations in which one finds oneself placed.

It might be noted in passing that in moving away from the ideal society, as outlined in *The Republic,* to that of the ordinary world as expounded in *The Laws,* Plato's thought bears a remarkable analogy to that of the early Fathers of the Church concerning the human condition before and after the Fall. A regularly recurrent theme in the writings of St. John Chrysostom, St. Ambrose and St. Jerome is that if man had not fallen the lineaments of society would be very different from what in fact they are. The State and law, in particular, would not exist, for men would not need such structures. Society would be very much what Toennies has called a "Gemeinschaft', unencumbered with "Gesellschaft" institutions. It would be free, spontaneous, charismatic, democratic, without any danger of degenerating into anarchy. Alas, original sin has excluded this and in his fallen state man needs law.

But to return to Plato's thought. Now that he had come to appreciate the need for a rule of law, he ambitioned drawing up as exhaustive a code as possible. Preliminary to this, he counselled an examination of the codes of other peoples, showing that the influence on him of Sophist empiricism was not entirely nil. But such fact-finding should merely serve as a guide to reason; Plato always remained the supreme rationalist. Laws—although framed by people well informed about the situation—must always be rationally established and have the force of reason. Their binding force must be ideas rather than facts. Because of this Plato emphasized the importance of preambles, by means of which laws are prefaced by the reasons which call for them. Here again one may notice the Socratic theme of virtue and knowledge being connected. If only one appreciated the reasons for a law, one would tend without further ado to observe it.

Such rationalism was a common characteristic of the Greeks. For Plato it meant that law, complete with pre-amble, was essentially a form of educational literature.

This had important and salutary implications for his idea of the basis of the duty to obey law. It was certainly not force of any kind, or any feeling of fear or negative guilt. Rather was it the moral worth of a man, in his own eyes and the eyes of society. Law gave him an idea of what he should do and should be; it presented him with a knowledge of himself.

How different this was from the stance of the Sophists, with their notions of law as something arbitrary and purely conventional, giving rise to a duty that rested solely on a basis of force and fear. How different even from some later presentations of Christian morals, which placed undue store on punishment for failure to conform. One feels in fact—and this is being said increasingly —that today we need an emphasis on moral motivation that is not unlike what Plato defended. We need an ethic of realization rather than of constraint.

In line with this, one does in fact notice the contemporary tendency towards taking pains to present the reasons for binding directives. It is a tendency common to the secular and the religious worlds. A good example in the latter is the encyclical *Humanae Vitae*, which spends so lengthy a time elaborating a concept of marriage from which to deduce the directives which follow. And it is notable that the majority of people who have contested these directives have done so on the basis of an alleged inadequacy in their supporting reasons.

To conclude with Plato's teaching on law and morality, we may recall simply its character of intrinsicality. Law is something given to be obeyed for itself; morality is something reasonable and realizable. Problems of all kinds there continue to be, especially that of how law might cater for individual situations. Plato did not succeed in solving this; Aristotle was to attempt to do so.

2

The Aristotelian Dilemma

AS IN THE case of the Sophists and that of Plato, some attention to Aristotle's methodology is a necessary antecedent to an understanding of his philosophy. And his general methodology is, in fact, a combination of Sophist empiricism and Platonic rationalism. Aristotle's logic united both. It was inductive, or empirical, in its framing of premises; deductive, or rational, in drawing the conclusions of syllogisms.

In matters of politics, law and ethics we get a particular application of this methodology to the domain of what Aristotle called practical knowledge. This division of knowledge into theoretical and practical is of supreme importance for proper scientific method, for it carried with it a correlative division of the sciences. Whereas the end or object of the theoretical sciences is truth, that of the practical sciences is action.

For Aristotle—as for all the ancient secular thinkers—legal and ethical science was a part of political. Indeed politics might be described as *the* practical science, covering everything that today is denoted by what are called the social sciences. In this Aristotle was in entire agreement with Plato—identifying the good of the individual with that of the State. But in one respect he differed notably—and decisively—from Plato in that he regarded the object of law as primarily action rather than knowledge in the sense of instruction. He did not quite partake of the view that knowledge *is* virtue.

In the strictest sense, for Aristotle, only the theoretical sciences—such as metaphysics, mathematics and the natural sciences—could properly be designated "science". The reason for this is that only these were regarded as constituting bodies of knowledge that are capable of being expressed by way of an orderly system of demonstrated syllogisms. In these fields only, he said, are premises so clearly true as to permit the drawing of apodictic conclusions. And only a body of such processes could constitute a science in the strictest sense of the term.

It will be immediately noticed how this Aristotelian concept of "science" differs from the modern concept which came in with Comte. For the latter all science had to follow the model of the physical sciences and had therefore to be confined to discovering measurable facts, establishing correlations or laws between sets of facts, and elaborating theories—or rather conceptual systems—within which the facts and the laws held together. As Comte saw things, science was nothing if not positive and enjoyed the certitude of incontestably proven physical facts and of ineluctably determined physical laws. This indeed is certitude with a vengeance.

Aristotle was not guilty of such *naïveté*. For him science was nothing if not rational, although, as previously indicated, this did not exclude a degree of empiricism. Important consequences flowed from this. In the first place, the notion of science as any rationally ordered body of knowledge left room within it for sciences whose subject matter cannot be touched by the experimental methods of science *à la* Comte. Ethics, as the science of values, is the prime example. For Comte there was no such thing; for Aristotle yes, in the domain of the practical sciences. In the second place, his notion of science allowed for varying degrees of certitude in relation to the precise subject matter being studied. There could be no question of attaining the same degree of accuracy in the science of ethics as is attainable in the natural sciences.

From this point of view the notion of practical science is important. It is undeniable that it was accepted as science by Aristotle, but in a loose sense such as today is applied to the human sciences, which are acknowledged to be inexact though scientific. The methodology of the practical sciences is not, and cannot be, exactly the same as that of the theoretical sciences. An immediate result is that one must not expect the same degree of precision in the practical as in the theoretical spheres. Nor should this be at all surprising, as scientific methodology and exactitude must vary in accordance with the subject matter studied. It is the mark of an educated mind, says Aristotle in the *Nicomachean Ethics*, to expect only that degree of certitude in a given subject matter as the nature of the subject matter permits.

Politics, ethics, law—these all fall into the category of science whose data must be somewhat imprecise. They deal with the subject of human action, but then in a sense there is no such thing but only actions of this or that kind. This action here and that action there has each its own exclusive dimension. Because they are free and therefore unpredictable, human actions pertain to the sphere of the contingent and to this extent are outside the realm of demonstration. The upshot in the field of political-legal-ethical science is that the only absolutely certain knowledge is that of general principles. The most famous of these is the Aristotelian ethical principle that virtue consists in a mean. Aristotle eschewed an approach to morals which would definitively prescribe that this or that concrete act is always right or wrong. In contrast with this, in the domain of theoretical knowledge, he issued precise directives in the *De Generatione et Corruptione*.

There is much in this that is relevant today. In particular, his division of science into theoretical and practical is something which can bear recalling. The basis for distinction which it provides between the human sciences and the physical sciences is of crucial import. It was due to forgetfulness of this distinction that the nineteenth century positivists thought that all science should have exactly the same methodology. It is due to forgetfulness of it also that certain moralists strive to develop incontrovertible and cocksure moral prescriptions, of the kind—once common in what came to be known as manuals of casuisty, but which are to be found too in textbooks of ethics—which construct thesis upon thesis complete with syllogistic method and accompanying scholions. And, finally, it is due to forgetfulness of it— at the other end of the spectrum—that moral science is sometimes criticized for not being sure enough in its findings and directives.

Aristotle's position, of course, can be pressed too far and this is done in fact by those moral, legal and political relativists for whom the principles of the practical sciences are universally pragmatic and perpetually revisable. Prominent among these are the exponents of *Situation Ethics*, according to which moral decisions can be made only by the individual conscience, in a context of ever-changing and non-repeatable sets of circumstances. Aristotle, while appreciative of the need to keep testing principles against life, was quite emphatic that there are certain principles—however few—whose validity is independent of practice. What is and what ought to be are logically different realities and one does not necessarily discover the one by examining the other. As later writers were to put it, the test of moral principles by facts must always remain a secondary criterion. We will return to this question again.

As with the Sophists and Plato, Aristotle's political philosophy was intimately related to his metaphysical persuasions. He too, in common with the other early Greek philosophers, was haunted by the problem of change. How is it that a thing can become something different while still remaining basically the same? For unless it remains, in some sense, throughout the process, there is question of a succession of annihilations and new creations rather than of mutation in the proper sense of the term.

The ancient world found this problem a difficult one. So difficult, in fact, that some thinkers maintained that there is really no such thing as change; it is something which seems to take place rather than truly does. Such were the views of Parmenides, the defender of one and permanent reality. In some ways this was not unlike the later position of Kant, for whom change pertained to the world of appearances, of *phenomena,* whereas the world of reality, of the *noumenon,* was constant. Quite opposed to the views of Parmenides were those of Heracleitus, for whom change was both the beginning and the end. There is nothing in being but flux, no substratum which endures throughout—a position not completely removed from what Hume put forward ages later when he denied the reality of substance and described being as a "phantasmagoria against a background of nothingness". This, of course, was really no explanation of change at all; like that of Parmenides, it was basically a denial of change.

It was in an effort to find a compromise in this very

controversy that Plato developed his theory of two worlds. On the one hand, there is the world of the many and the changing, on the other, that of the one and the permanent. The latter is the realm of abstract ideas about which we have written already when dealing with his treatment of justice.

Respectful though he was towards Plato, Aristotle was aware that this too was no solution to the problem of change. For change involves permanence in its warp and woof, and to separate its two aspects—something which ceases and something which continues—is to fail to face up to the challenge of change. Change takes place in one and the same world, in one and the same thing which is changing. Aristotle's own contribution to explaining the nature of change was the elaboration of the theory of Hylemorphism. Change, he said, is a succession of "forms" against a primordial ground of "matter". The form is that which makes anything what it is; it is in fact the "idea" of that thing. When its form, its idea, changes, a different entity has come into being. But, in the case of material things, something always remains throughout the change. This in fact is what makes them material and this is what Aristotle called prime matter. A piece of wood that has been burned is no longer wood but ashes; a new form or idea has replaced the old. Yet there is question not of entire disappearance and new replacement but of something going and coming and something remaining. Thus, in Aristotle, Plato's "ideas", while continuing to be relevant, were brought down to earth and incarnated in material reality.

In the case of living things, change takes on a special dimension which is better termed development than change. In these it is the form which organizes their growth; it is the idea—the "nature"—which determines them internally and brings each to its proper perfection.

3

Here we touch on Aristotle's doctrine of the four "causes" of being, the four roots of its rational comprehension. First of all, there is the "material" cause, or that out of which a thing is made. Secondly, there is its "formal" cause, that which makes it to be what it is. Then there is the efficient cause or what brought it into existence and, lastly, the final cause, its *raison d'être*, its purpose or end in being. This was a fruitful approach and in later history it did yield much fruit, when Aristotelian ideas were worked over again by the Schoolmen. Aristotle himself never carried it to full fruition. On the material cause he wrote extensively, but seems to have failed to reap the full riches of the concept of efficient causality. Had he done so, he would have graduated from the notion of contingency to that of the absolute in a process of intellection whose ultimate term would have been God. He failed to do this, leaving himself with puzzles, as we shall shortly see, even in the domain of morality.

About the formal cause Aristotle wrote well, and in the case of living things especially so. It is the formal cause which constitutes the idea or nature of an organism and which is responsible, by way of an internal influence, for its development. In a sense, in fact, it exercises a kind of efficient causality but even more so, it is a final cause. For it is its idea or nature that represents an organism's full capacity for development and that draws it towards this by its teleological force. With the exception of Democritus and the Sophists, the Greeks were rationalists. Is it not they who laid the foundations of our Western intellectual tradition? They believed that the problems of existence were capable of solution, for they assumed— and can one do more than either assume it or refuse to do so?—that existence had a meaning, that is, a purpose. Purpose or finality goes hand in hand with rationalism, in the sense, that is, of a proferring of conceptual explanations to the many-faceted problem of being. There was no place for chance in Aristotle's universe, supreme intellectual that he was. Things are what they are and move towards what they are capable of being in virtue of their idea or nature, which is something conceptual and therefore rational. And one can discover what this is, by examining their activity in an analytic process of rational intellection.

Man, like other animals, undergoes a process of development, whereby his nature can be brought to full perfection. But it is not a wholly determined sort of thing as is the instinctive development of irrational animals. Man's glory is that he is an intelligent and free being; in Sartre's language he can make his own world; he is largely in control of his personal destiny. Hence it is that man perfects himself by way of free activity, an activity which realizes the implications of his nature to the full—of his form, his essence, his idea as man, in other words, his humanity.

One should note well that Aristotle thought—as did the rest of antiquity—that this accomplishment is impossible to the isolated individual. Only a beast, who is less than man, or a God, who is more than man, can develop himself outside the pale of society. Outside the pale of the *polis*, in fact, because for all practical purposes the only society which counted was political society or the City-State. It is for this reason that Aristotle defined man as a *zoon politicon*, i.e. a political animal. He needs life in the State if he is to develop his full potentialities, to bring out all that is entailed by his nature, his full and complete meaning as man. Just as the womb is a necessary environment for the development of the physical aspects of the embryo, so the State is necessary for the development of the spiritual aspect of man which is manifested by and enshrined in his conduct.

For Aristotle, as for all who partook of his vision, law

is the instrument of politics. Law it is that provides the framework—the social atmosphere—which enables man to develop his nature. As States differ, so do their citizens, and not as citizens only but as men. There is a sea fish, known as *fundulus,* which, if hatched out in normal water, is endowed with the usual two eyes. In certain chemically treated water he would emerge with one eye. In much the same way, for Aristotle, the nature of man is inextricably linked with his socio-political context. And thus can differ from State to State. I suppose nowadays sociologists and anthropologists would say the same thing through the medium of the concept of cultural variation.

Whatever of this, for Aristotle the role of the State and the law of the State was pivotal to the development of man, including his moral dimension. Curiously enough, in view of this, in Aristotle as in Plato one finds no explicit treatment of the notion of law. What one does find are a number of reflections on law in the general context of his writing on justice.

In the *Ethics* the idea of justice is distinguished into "general" and "particular", the former of which is again divided into "absolute" and "political". The notion of particular justice does not concern us here; it is the kind of justice which was later to be termed a cardinal virtue. General justice represents the Platonic notion of virtue in general, *dikaiosyné* or righteousness. As "absolute" justice it is viewed, as it were, in the abstract; as "political" justice it is viewed as incarnate in this or that State.

At this point a further distinction in political justice is introduced, viz. between "natural" and "legal" justice. For the moment, it will suffice to say that natural justice derives from the natural order and legal justice from conventional precepts. But, whether it be natural or conventional, political justice for Aristotle derives entirely from the law of the State.

In short, for Aristotle the positive law of the State—positive, that is, in the sense of being enacted and enforced by man—is composed of two elements, one discovered, the other decided. The discovered, or given, element springs from the purely natural order, the decided, or constructed, element from purely positive choice. But these elements are by no means completely distinct, nor different *inter se*, and certainly never opposed one to the other. The purely positive element is itself natural after a fashion. This is because of Aristotle's special conception of "nature" as both something given to and something constructed by man, i.e. something in the growth of which man cooperates by a continuous process of the addition of artificial elements.

Nobody has written more clearly about this than has Sir Ernest Barker, in his introduction to Gierke's classical treatise *Natural Law and the Theory of Society* (Cambridge 1934):

> In Aristotle's general terminology the word "natural" as applied to man and human things, has three senses. It is something which is immanent in the primordial constitution of man, as a potentiality for development. Again it is something which has developed with his development . . . . a growth in which his art or creative mind has co-operated with . . . . his instinct . . . . . Finally, it is something which is inherent in the final development of man and part of his final cause or purpose . . . . . All three senses are interconnected in virtue of the idea of development. If we take them all into consideration we shall see that a "natural" law will not merely mean a law which is co-extensive with man, or universal; it will also mean a law which has grown concurrently with man . . . . (and with which) man's art has co-operated in its growth. The anti-

thetics between natural and conventional which is only a *prima facie* antithesis will disappear.

The later tendency to view the artificial as in some way unnatural was absolutely alien to Aristotelian thought. Without question, of course, if it were out of harmony with the nature of man as a capacity for development, the artificial could not be regarded as natural. The primordial idea of man with its implicit potentialities constitutes his basic nature which must be respected by being actualized. Its actualization, however, is compatible with—indeed demands—creative effort on his part, by which an extension of his being is achieved through what he constructs. Man grows in stature, not just by giving rein to his instincts but by moulding his conduct and the integument thereto. This integument is the physical and social framework of his life, the fabricated environment which we call culture. To the extent that one man's culture differs from that of another, to that extent there is some difference between them as men. Some difference, that is, in nature. At the primordial level they are universally the same but have undergone a process of evolution along somewhat different lines. Any process that is incompatible with the original datum would, needless to say, not qualify for being regarded as natural. Each man in his own way seeks a full development, but the end product will be analogical rather than univocal insofar as cultural differences are consolidated and perpetuated.

Hence it is that in constructing a body of conventional precepts for conduct, men engage in developing the natural. What are therefore called purely positive laws are in this respect a determination of natural law. But both together —whether given or constructed—are presented to men by the positive law of the State. So much so that, for simplicity, one could say that, according to the Aristotelian way of looking at things, the natural law and the law of the State were one and the same thing.

Heinrich Rommen has put the position well in his book
The Natural Law (St. Louis, 1947):

> The natural law does not dwell in a region beyond
> the positive law. The natural law has to be realised
> in the positive law, since the latter is the application
> of the universal idea of justice to the motley mani-
> fold of life. The immutable idea of right dwells in
> the changing positive law. All positive law is the
> more or less successful attempt to realise the natural
> law.

It is not necessary to look beyond the law of the State
—the positive law—to secure a knowledge of the natural
law. One is reminded by this of the general thesis advanced by Bishop Robinson of Woolwich to the effect that
God and God's law are not to be sought after "out there"
but rather "in here". The difference between the two
lies in the fact that, whereas the bishop claims that morality stems from the dictates of the individual conscience, for
Aristotle it stems from the positive law of the State.

Between its given and constructed elements the law of
the State represents the entire moral order. It is a rule
of law that is completely human whether in being discovered or decided—in one way or another the product
of reason. And it is the instrumental framework within
which men can be virtuous. The State exists to bring
about the good life. The good life is life in accordance
with virtue, that is, general justice. General justice finds
concrete expression in political justice, of which the law
of the State is the instrument. Hence morality—natural
morality—is capable of achievement by man by observing
the law of the State as a good citizen.

It is very apparent that God is not the author and
giver of the Rule of Law as conceived by Aristotle. As

already mentioned, his reference to the gods in the *Ethics* conduces no more than to the framing of a hypothesis. His celestial Prime Mover was certainly not God in the usual sense of the term. At most it was but the posited ground of the cosmological mechanism, lacking personality and the capacity for interest in man's activity. In such a deistic universe there was no possibility of reward for the just man in an after life. The last end of man must be in the here and now, and Aristotle did view things thus. Just as the sculptor etc. have each an end or purpose, so also does man as such. Aristotle believed that it consisted in happiness, which—theoretically at least—should follow on the living of the good life, from observing the law and perfecting his nature. The truth, unfortunately, is not always so. Aristotle was well aware of the many just men who were unhappy, the victims of misfortune of one kind or another. The State is not always able to ensure their happiness. Is unhappiness then always to be their lot? Aristotle could never get to the bottom of this problem. For him it constituted the great dilemma, a dilemma indeed that was felt by many of the ancients, the dilemma of the good pagan's failure. The Stoics, as we shall see, were to make a stout effort to solve it, but it was not squarely faced until the advent of Christianity. "Thou hast made us for thyself, O Lord", St. Augustine was to write, "and our hearts are ever restless until they rest in thee".

There was another dilemma also from which Aristotle did not escape, the dilemma of how to deal with contingent situations characterized by circumstances which the law could not envisage. Not that law could not prescribe concerning rather detailed personal matters; the identity of Ethics and Politics made this a matter of course. It could prescribe, for example, the conduct of the brave man (not to desert), that of the temperate man (not to commit adultery), that of the gentleman (not to assault or abuse others). The negative approach to these prescriptions is worth pondering over for a moment, as it is linked with an important quality of law as elaborated by Aristotle and also Plato. Plato too had suggested a codification of law by asking what pleasures should not be enjoyed and correlatively what pains should not be avoided? How different an approach from seeking to specify positively what should be done. To attempt this would be to risk an omnicompetence and authoritarianism that would suffocate the liberty of man. As Karl Rahner has said somewhere, even the Church is not entitled to specify in concrete detail the entire content of our spiritual life, say to the extent of exclusively prescribing what prayers we should say in the morning. This would be ecclesiastical totalitarianism. Aristotle avoided something similar in his City-State *cum* Church by counselling that law should largely be a system which excluded certain modes of conduct while leaving it to the citizens to decide positively what to do. It could thus be quite detailed from one point of view while at the same time avoiding infringement of their personal liberty.

But from another point of view it was not detailed enough. For law of its very nature must deal with the average man and ignore the concrete problems of the individual. There is need therefore for some added factor which will discover when the letter of the law is inadequate if applied woodenly to the case of the individual. This is what has traditionally been known as equity or *epikeia*—regarded as a virtue in fact which enables a man to know what to do in particular situations when the justice of the letter of the law would be too harsh. The big trouble about this is that it expects the individual to fall back on himself in those circumstances in which the legislator, if he were aware of the problem, would be quite prepared to grant a dispensation. As Plato had learned, so also Aristotle knew that it is impossible for the ruler to be thus omnipresent. Willy-nilly the individual citizen is left on his own resources. In Aristotle's view, however, these resources were inadequate as far as the mass of the citizens were concerned. As he saw things, if the average citizen were capable of knowing what to do in exceptional cases, *a fortiori* he should know what to do in the generality. This would be to assume that he is capable of being his own legislator, something from which Aristotle forever shied away.

As the *Ethics* and the *Politics* make abundantly clear, only the philosopher is capable of legislating. The ruling class constitute an *élite,* through whose good offices it is open to others to become perfect. Indeed the theoretical reason for Aristotle's identification of morality with obedience to the law of the State, was precisely the need of the ordinary citizen for a sociological framework which would underpin his efforts to work out his earthly salvation. It is a viewpoint which finds a certain resonance even in Christianity. Readers of Danielou's book *Prayer as a Political Problem* will remember how he emphasizes the fact that not all Christians belong to the kind of *élite* that need no support for their religion from sociological structures. To expect the majority of them to work out their salvation by way of a socially unaided personal response—against a background of a pure intellectual and ascetical appreciation of the issues—would be as unrealistic as to expect the mass of men to appreciate contemporary abstract art rather than the more homely variety of previous ages. A point may be reached in some remote and Teilhardian future when the common man will cease to be common. In the meantime in his religious life he needs popular art and popular devotions, and—as far as he can get it—a socio-political infrastructure such as will promote rather than impede his religious aspirations.

In his own way Aristotle was saying much the same

kind of thing when he declared the mass of the citizen body incapable of legislating for themselves in such a way as to know what to do in concrete situations. From which sprang his further dilemma as to how to secure the equitable in practice? To get over the difficulty he relied on the ruling *élite* to apply something like the rules of construction used by judges. Surely, he said, by way of example, a man found guilty of striking another while wearing a ring, should not be held to have broken a law against using a metal weapon.

This solution was specious rather than real. For in handing over the ensuring of equity to the ruler in this way, was Aristotle implying that equity itself is governed by rules? If so cannot it also become rigid and inflexible; if not, does not justice cease to be uniform? Rules of construction are insufficient to meet the problem. In the case of the ring, for instance, there could be a big debate as to whether the kind of ring in question could be relevant to deciding whether it should be classified as a metal weapon. A big enough ring could be tantamount to a knuckle-duster and there is a type of ring said to be worn nowadays by criminals and secret agents which, on pressing a spring, discloses a small switch-blade.

Aristotle never solved the problem of how to ensure equity. It is, he said,

> something of a problem . . . . . The equitable, while it is something better than one sort of just, is none the less still just; and if it is better than the just, it is not in the sense of being a different class of thing. The just and the equitable belong to one class; both are good, but the equitable is the better. What creates the problem is the fact that the equitable, though it is just, is not legally just. On the contrary it is by its nature a corrective of the legally just.
> (*Nicomachean Ethics*, Bk. 5)

Although he did not realize it, Aristotle here was under-lining the impossibility of completely identifying morality and legality. He had unintentionally provided eloquent evidence that there is more to natural law than what is contained in the positive law of the State.

Another way of saying the same thing is that the notion of conscience as such played no part in the thought of Aristotle. Most likely because the concept of moral responsibility—related to "duty"—was practically un-known to the ancient world. There was a world of dif-ference between the moral system of the Greeks and ours, due mainly to their different world outlook. It is true, as Arthur Adkins has pointed out in his *Merit and Re-sponsibility: A Study in Greek Values* (Oxford, 1960), that Aristotle did have some concept of responsibility in the sense of acting with a full understanding of the nature of one's action. But this was less conscientious action as commonly understood than enlightened behaviour de-liberately chosen as the expression of a settled policy. As such it was something that was possible only to the more active and decisive men; it was entirely foreign to the common run of humanity. The *areté* or virtue of the ordinary Greek was inimical to the concept of moral responsibility. It was something passive and co-operative rather than decisive.

As a result, it is perhaps not surprising that Aristotle should have regarded happiness also as possible only to the citizens proper. It cannot be ambitioned by the artisan class who are not capable of exercising responsibility and cultivating virtue. For even though in the *Politics* virtue is looked upon as being achieved in and through the community, and in Ethics (*Nicomachean Ethics*, Bk. X) it is equally clear that contemplation (*theoria*) on the part of the individual is the highest virtue (*areté*) of all, it is qualitatively different from the practical activity of the rank and file.

The central meaning of it all is that, in the Aristotelian system of things, while virtue entailed happiness it was the happiness of a few, an earthly beatitude attainable only by an *élite*. There was no question of a moral responsibility on the part of all men such as could lead all to virtue and its reward. For this it was necessary as a preliminary step that some concept of conscience be worked out, a concept which implies some element of a consciousness of the transcendental, leading ultimately in Christianity to a responsibility in the sense of "the condition of a free being under obligation, a being whose freedom and obligation are both due to his creation and vocation by God" (Albert R. Jonsen, *Responsibility in Modern Religious Ethics*, Washington, 1968, p. 17). This adds to the notion of obedience not only that of deliberate consideration but that of subjection to a rule of law that is above the world of man even while pertaining to it.

In the *Nicomachean Ethics* (Bk. III, C.5) Aristotle wrote: "Because each man is in a sense responsible for his moral dispositions, he will also be responsible for his conception of the good; otherwise no man would be responsible for his own evil deeds". Inversely, it would seem true to say that the concept of responsibility of Aristotelian man was severely limited by his conception of the good.

3

Order in Stoic Perspectives

THE STOICS were among the first to use the term "natural law", beginning with Zeno around the year 300 B.C. Their philosophy—Stoicism—had a long innings, persevering into and flourishing during Roman times. Among its best known adherents were Chrysippus, Epictetus, Marcus Aurelius and Cicero.

The general approach of the Stoics to law is perhaps best exemplified by Chrysippus in a passage from his treatise *On Law*: "Law is the ruler of all things divine and human, the settled arbiter of good and evil, the guide to justice and injustice, the sovereign Lord of all who are by nature political animals. It directs what must be done and forbids the opposite".

Here there is an amalgam of ideas which bring together almost everything that had been said about law in the past. Materially at least the idea of Pindar is there, that law is something divine; so too is that of Aristotle that it is something human. And very much there is present the king-pin of all ancient thought about justice, namely, that law is that which moulds the conduct of social beings. Even though Chrysippus was writing not more than a hundred years after the time of Aristotle, he no longer conceived justice as centred on the former *polis* or on the positive human law of same. His thought, in essence, is not at all Aristotelian in flavour; its perspectives are considerably broader. Law, while human, is not exclusively a human thing, nor is it expressed simply by the laws of the State. Rather is it something coterminous with society as such, the universal touchstone of the justice of all men. The *cosmopolis* had replaced the *polis*.

There were two reasons for this change of perspective. First of all, there was the policy of Alexander the Great, from 325 on, which encouraged the unity of the Macedonians and Persians in one empire. Gone were the days of the many and small Greek City-States, each with its own law and pattern of justice. The inclusion of the Persians—the *barbaroi* of previous ages—with the Greeks in one system meant that its social structure had to be radically different from that of the *polis*. Its broad lines had to be cosmopolitan or universal rather than local or provincial in their orientation. In the second place, and this was true more especially in the later Roman period, the quality of political life had deteriorated. Under despotic and crazy Caesars the idea that justice stemmed from the State became more and more difficult to swallow. It was against this background that the Stoic idea emerged that the truly just man was a citizen of the world rather than of any State. He was one who was guided by a universal natural law that was really distinct from positive human law. *"Non scripta sed nata lex"*, said Cicero, meaning that man has an inborn notion of right and wrong.

One of the most moving and fecund descriptions of this natural law has come down to us in a fragment of Cicero's lost treatise *De Republica,* reproduced fortunately in quotation by Lactantius. Law, says Cicero,

> is of universal application, unchanging and everlasting . . . . . It is a sin to try to alter this law, nor is it allowable to try to repeal any part of it, and it is impossible to abolish it. We cannot be freed from its obligations by senate or people . . . . . There shall no longer be one law at Rome, another at Athens, one law today, another tomorrow; but the same Law, everlasting and unchangeable, shall bind all nations and all times. And there shall be one master and ruler, that is, God, over us all for He is the author of this Law, its promulgator and its enforcing judge. And he who will not obey shall be an exile from himself, and, despising his own humanity shall in that very act, suffer the greatest of all punishments which can be imagined.

The end of this passage is particularly illuminating, for it shows the extent to which the era of the City-State had come to an end. No longer is exile from the *polis* the greatest evil that can befall a human being. And basically the reason is that he is no longer thought of in the old sense as a "political animal". He is a social animal—a member of the human community—of humanity, and the most severe disaster which he can suffer is to become alienated from this through injustice, through ignoring the law of man as man, the law of humanity as such. The concept of physical exile has been replaced by that of psychological alienation and the general perspective has become more spiritual in tone.

We get a more concrete examination of law in Cicero's *De Legibus.* Here we find a threefold classification of law into the *Lex Coelestis,* the *Lex Naturae* and the

Lex Vulgus. The *Lex Coelestis*—or Heavenly Law—is a sort of absolute standard, something like Aristotle's absolute justice had been. The *Lex Naturae,* as its name indicates, is what we call Natural Law, while the *Lex Vulgus* is purely positive human prescription.

Speaking of the *Lex Coelestis,* Cicero observes that it is the opinion of the wisest men that, fundamentally, law is not to be thought of as simply a product of human thought. We note here an immediate contrast with Aristotle. Whereas Aristotle worked towards a kind of *rapprochement* between law in general and positive human decree, Cicero sought a *rapprochement* between law and divine decree. Law, he maintained, has an element in it that is eternal. It rules the universe, which is why it is said to be the mind of God.

At first sight it would appear that now the human aspect of law has become completely overshadowed by that of the divine. That this is not quite so, however, becomes apparent on closer inspection of the general Stoic outlook. What exactly did Cicero mean when he said that law *is* the mind of God? It is possible that he was referring to an earlier utterance of the Platonic Socrates, who spoke of the human ruler as capable of legislating in virtue of his *daimones*. Many essays have been written in interpretation of what precisely might have been meant by this. Despite the more simplistic of these attempts, it would seem to be mistaken to identify the *daimones* with subordinate gods. Rather were they sparks of the divine, in the sense of the human mind or reason viewed as a divine thing. The divine and human were therefore in a sense interfused.

The Stoics spoke of the mind as the *logos,* the word or root of idea. And they looked upon it as incarnate in nature. That is to say, the material and bodily world is interpenetrated with that of the spirit, of idea. This is an entirely pantheistic understanding of being, whereby God

4

and nature were closely identified. The *logos* is the high point of the evolution of being, the culmination of nature in divine self-consciousness. The individual man, through his reason, participates in the reason of the universe, in the divine idea or plan of existence. Or to put the matter shortly and starkly, nature is God and reason Fate. The most that reason can do is to appreciate the "reasons" why nature develops as it does. Through reason, as it were, man gets at least a limited glimpse of the inner workings of the self-unfolding being of God, who is at once material being and rational idea.

There are fascinating points of contrast and comparison between these concepts and others both pagan and Christian. One might note, for instance, the role played by the "idea" in Cicero as against that which it plays in Plato and Aristotle. For Plato, as we have seen, it was accessible only in another world, by means of a kind of mystical intuition. For Aristotle its unveiling was a matter for rational analysis whereby *form* was disengaged from *matter* in an exclusively human world. Cicero and the Stoics introduced a *tertium quid* by their incarnation of the idea in nature. The *logos,* the mind of God, through the instrumentality of man's mind, became conscious of the idea or reason in being. It was a process neither of mystical intuition nor of rational analysis but of an inner insight or contemplation.

There is comparison and contrast also between Stoic ideas and those of Christianity. The doctrine of the incarnate Word in the prologue of the Gospel of St. John is the best-known point of comparison. But it is also a point of contrast due to its theist rather than pantheist perspectives. For the Stoics, humanity and the divine are drawn together by an intermingling in the warp and woof of nature. Christianity brings them together too but in a different way. Nature, as such, is not divine; on the contrary it is defective and in need of redemption. This has been made possible to it by the incarnation of the Word, through whom all things can return to God. In truth, "in Him we live and move and have our being" and to Him we are destined to return. For men are intended to "be like gods". Nor is our humanity to be despised in the process, as the Neo-Platonists would have us believe. It is true that, at times, in the writings of St. Paul, we do come across some bald utterances. One such is where he advises Christians to seek the things of heaven in preference to those of earth. For their interests, as Christians, are in heaven. These passages go down badly at the present time when so much emphasis is being placed on humanism. Indeed, use has been made of them by existentialists like Sartre and Merleau-Ponty to demonstrate the incompatability of Christianity and humanism. The truth of course is extremely different. The pivotal meaning of the Incarnation is the possibility of humanism by way of a purified and uplifted nature— a nature transformed by Grace. It has always been Christian teaching that grace does not destroy nature but perfects it.

There are also points of resemblance, yet with many and profound differences, between the Stoic concept of fate and that of Christian providence. To the Stoic the workings of nature represented a remorseless grinding out of the self-revelation of the being of God. The best that man could do was to accept it "stoically", that is, as something inevitable. The Christian concept of providence introduces a different dimension when it speaks of man's "duty" to accept the "will of God". For Christianity, it is not so much a question of developing a rational acquiescence to an inescapable chain of events, as of voluntarily accepting the plan of a creator God, who is distinct from his creatures, including man. Which means that Christianity respected human liberty in a way that Stoicism did not, and in a way that has also been forgotten by those atheist existentialists who keep telling us that the Christian religion is incompatible with human liberty, in the sense of man's creative historicity in making his own world.

In the *De Legibus,* by way of a dialogue, Cicero asks his brother Quintus to explain further the idea of law as the reason of God. And so he does, after the manner of the passage quoted from the *De Republica.* The key idea is that the author of the law is both God and humanity—the pantheistic system which we have been endeavouring to explain. In this context, one finds it easier to understand the full implications of the idea that disregard for the law makes a man an exile from himself. Such exile becomes a much more terrible thing than exile from society and the protection which its gods had to offer. In the pantheistic context of man as the end of man, exile from humanity meant the loss of "salvation". In this respect there is a world of difference between the immanentism of Stoicism and the transcendentalism of Christian teaching.

One of the best expositions of this Stoic-Christian relationship which I know, occurs in Alain Hus's book *Greek and Roman Religion* (London, 1962). An extended quotation may therefore be in order:

The Stoics believed that the world was a universal city governed by a power called Fate, Zeus, Providence or Nature, which was, in short, God. From this God, who was material, came the four primitive elements—fire, air, earth and water—and all that exists in the world, including the soul of man. So everything came from God and everything was God. The world, having come from God, was to be absorbed back into God . . . . . There was thus a divine plan for the universe, and God was the universal Law whose decrees rule the world.

The lot of man was thus determined, for God was Fate. But he was also Reason, and all that he decided was just . . . . . Since the soul was part of God, all men were equal and brothers in spirit . . . . . By using his reason, man ought to move towards a greater resemblance to God . . . . . Thus the progress of the sage was set out: he had to apply himself to the knowledge of God and of himself, and to the practice of virtue (submission to universal Reason), and this was true happiness. What other happiness for a divine soul could there be than its self-accomplishment?

So (in a sense) the ideas of duty and conscience were developed along with those of universal brotherhood and the advance towards God, bringing Stoicism nearer to Christian ideas. The vision of a divine plan for the world, and the emphasis placed on the soul . . . . are further elements of Stoic teaching which, looked at somewhat loftily, gave rise later to the hypothesis that Seneca had met St. Paul—a hypothesis with no solid foundation.

But let us make no mistake about it. Stoicism and Christianity did not spring from the same spirit, had different cardinal virtues, and addressed themselves to different souls. Stoicism remained the philosophy of an élite; it never found its way into men's hearts, or brought any relief to the sufferings of the humble. It left ordinary men with no sure hope for the after-life. If some thinkers grafted on to Stoic teachings belief in the immortality of the soul in the heavens, nothing was officially said about the lot of the soul (divine, but material) after death. No hope of any *post mortem* retribution came to humanize what was always an austere intellectual kind of wisdom.

Thus it was that Stoicism also failed to escape from the basic dilemma of pagan antiquity.

When the earliest Stoics, like Zeno, spoke of law they had spoken only of one Law—the *Lex Coelestis*. They declined to proceed to an elaboration of its content by the construction of any concrete body of law. They were "citizens of the world" in the purest sense, to the extent in fact of ignoring States and civil laws. They remind one of the sophisticated and cosmopolitan Germans of the pre-Fichte era who would describe themselves before all else as Europeans. Or of the international set of the present day who owe devoted allegiance to no State and whose juridical principles are enshrined in the Universal Declaration of the Rights of Man of the United Nations and applied at the level of the world court at the Hague. For the early Stoics there was no need for any courts. Zeno in fact sought their abolition altogether and their replacement by the freedom of the *Lex Coelestis*. Once again, one is tempted to draw an analogy between this and "the freedom of the sons of God" spoken of by St. Paul. In the *First Epistle to the Corinthians* the letter says that Christians should refrain as much as possible from engaging in lawsuits.

Unlike Zeno, Cicero was a practical lawyer as well as a philosopher and went on to give more concrete meaning to the *Lex Coelestis*. There are also laws, he said, that are designed by peoples to meet what appear to be perennial needs of man. All peoples everywhere have introduced institutions concerning property, concerning marriage and the family, the use of force and so on. These institutions—factors of order or legal arrangements —can vary from place to place and time to time. Modern cultural anthropologists know exactly the extent of this variation in all domains. To take just one example, that of ensuring peace in the community. Among the more primitive inhabitants of New Guinea it is ensured by means of the Kula system which establishes a cross-pattern of friendships by the exchange of token gifts. In other societies fear is employed through the agency of groups for the punishing of miscreants, after a manner which, however much it may resemble lynch law, is in reality highly controlled, accepted by and under the sanction of the community. A cross-cultural perspective makes one realize quickly that social stability does not depend exclusively on legislative, judicial and executive organs of western vintage. The helmeted "bobbies" of Victorian England would be less effective in Polynesia than the grass-skirted "bull-roarer" enforcers of order whose efficiency depends largely on their powers of menace.

What is noticeable the world over is that there are certain common values which all peoples strive to institutionalize. The forms of institutionalism can vary but the basic values are common to all. With few exceptions, such as hippie communes which only serve to prove the rule, all peoples are agreed on the institution of marriage. The form, however, can be monogamous or polygamous and be surrounded by an immense variety of customs. It was the residual element which Cicero had in mind when he noted that all peoples have certain common values which they seek to institutionalize. These institutions incarnate, represent, express the *Lex Coelestis* in so far as it concerns the free conduct of man. They constitute what he called the *Lex Naturae*, or natural law, which is the *Lex Coelestis* as it applies to this sphere.

It was this concept that was taken up by Roman jurists like Scaevola, Calpurnius, Gaius and Ulpian, and its content developed by way of an entire code of law governing marriage and the family, property, etc. Thereby there emerged the idea of a law of peoples or States that was not the law simply of this or that State only but something basically common to all and therefore natural to man. It was Cicero who coined the term *Jus Gentium* to describe this, meaning a sort of World Common Law for all men. True to his pantheism he regarded it as something more than human in its origin, but it was also human and hence had to cater for human differences. While one and the same for all in essence, in form it was flexible and somewhat mutable.

Mutable, however, only up to a point. Cicero was aware that from time to time people seek to institutional-ize the basic values along lines that in reality do not serve them. Certain marriage customs turn out to be perverse, certain practices in wartime inhuman. Mindful of this, he said that laws can rightly be called law only when they are just, i.e. in accordance with the primal standard. Wicked laws should not be called "laws" nor wicked law-givers "rulers"—no more than ignorant persons who prescribe poisons should be dignified with the title "physicians". The primal standard of nature must always be respected when formulating the concrete shape of institutions. Just as animals conform to this by blind instinct—implanted in them by the divine mind—so man should conform to the order of the universe by way of his reason—the divine mind implanted in him. He does so through the creation of structures, of institutions, which though varied in form are one in purpose. And the simplest way of establishing what is acceptable to nature is to consult what has been done by the common consent of men.

The notion of the common consent of men as a criterion of morality has appeared again and again in the field of ethics since. The Scholastics and their successors were never in doubt that it constituted a secondary and manifestative criterion reflecting the primary and con-stitutive criterion of nature. The Scholastics likewise accepted the linked notion of the *Law of Nations*, or *Lex Gentium* as St. Thomas Aquinas was to call it.

Indeed, as we shall presently see, the latter identified what he called the secondary precepts of the natural law with the corpus of precepts that constitute the *Law of Nations*. The primary precepts of the natural law were those basic elementary values which for Cicero, went to constitute the natural law as he understood it.

I think it fair to say that, during its later period, Scholasticism somewhat overlooked the flexibility of the secondary principles of the natural law. In general, as we shall see, the great weight of emphasis was on the immutability of natural law as linked with divine law. Unlike the Stoic concept to which it owed so much, natural law in the late Scholastic period tended to forget that, as the *Law of Nations*, it is actually enshrined in the laws and customs of peoples insofar as these are institutionalizations of universal values.

To forget this was also to forget another aspect of Stoic thought which is of considerable importance for all legal theory. I mean the role of the community in the formulation of law. For law is indeed an analogous entity; it includes customs and mores as much as precepts. Under some of its forms—notably custom—the role of the community is quite evident, but it is a role which should never be entirely absent from law-making. Realism suggests that the sociological perspective of community reaction should at least be taken into account by the lawgiver. The Stoics were really stressing this when they conceived the natural law, within the *Law of Nations*, as the common consent of mankind regarding certain values. And when allowing for flexibility in the matter of institutionalizing these values, they were again giving due place to community considerations in gearing customs and precepts to suit the appropriate circumstances. All this has assumed a new interest today, when anthropological evidence of differing mores is mounting and when no one in his senses would dream of framing a universal system of law which would neglect adaptation to varying social requirements. One may remark in passing that the Stoic attention to the function of the community in the sphere of law, is paralleled today by the emphasis in the Church on the role of the community in ecclesiastical decisions.

Passing now to the *Lex Vulgus*, it was Cicero's view that this is simply the naked positive law, entirely conventional and arbitrary. It is whatever decrees are in written form by the simple method of command or prohibition. It has no necessary reference to the primal standard of nature; it can accidentally coincide with this, but even when contrary to it, is called law. This, he said, is the crowd's notion, the popular or vulgar concept of law. Hence the name which he chose to give it. He dismissed the concept as valueless from the point of view of the philosophy of law but had to include reference to it if his treatment of law was to be complete. One remark which he made about it is, however, important. This is that, insofar as it includes precepts that are clearly unjust, it is not really law at all. One is reminded forcibly of St. Thomas Aquinas's later well-known dictum: *Lex injusta non est lex sed legis corruptio.*

Cicero admitted nevertheless that, unjust "laws" excluded, the *Lex Vulgus* can have a practical use. The reason is that not everyone can be a member of the *élite* who will succeed in unveiling the natural law for themselves. In this he was more down to earth than Zeno and the early Stoics for whom the idea of justice seemed to be sufficient to secure its application. In the nineteenth century one had such views among the Utopian Socialists, as Saint-Simon, Owen, Fourier and Proudhon. Engels came to realize their impractical character, "cobweb spinning flea crackers" as he picturesquely called them. Long before then Plato had abandoned the communism of his *Republic* for a more work-a-day arrangement of things. Fourier's *phalanstéres* and Owen's communes were all to go a similar road. So too were Saint-Simon's and Proudhon's lofty ideas concerning the accessibility and the force of the concept of justice as far as the man in the street is concerned. An *élite,* pagan or Christian, might well get on without positive law; the mass of men certainly cannot.

Positive laws, however, should be just, by being in accordance with reason, with nature. And basic justice as Cicero was very much aware, is the same for all men and human societies. He was also aware that this is not self-evident, because what goes as justice varies in place and time. This awareness created a problem for Cicero, a problem which under another form we have also seen to exercise Aristotle, the problem of the one and the many in the field of the just, of the general norm and the contingent exception. It is surprising how this same problem, under one guise or another, keeps continually cropping up over the course of history. Today's debate concerning a universal morality or a morality of situations, is only a variation of this age-old theme.

In his *De Republica* Cicero teased the problem out by examining Carneades' argument to the effect that justice is mere convention. Carneades is being used as a kind of *advocatus diaboli,* an exponent in the Sophist tradition of why laws can vary from place to place and time to time, even in respect of one and the same thing. Surely this could not be if justice were uniform? If justice were a product of nature it would be always the same, like hot and cold, whereas, in truth, it is anything but this. In Rome the gods are worshipped as human in form; in Egypt they are worshipped as animals. More to the point is the example that the Romans deem stealing dishonourable, whereas for the Cretans the profession of piracy is a noble one. Similarly, there are differing laws concerning the place and role of women—and so the list could go on. Are all of these provisions equally just? If not, how does one know which are?

Cicero's answer to this is available to us only in part, by way of the reproduction by Lactantius of part of the lost *De Republica*. And, in so far as it goes, it seems to be really a denial of the problem, a running away from facing up to the issues. Cicero says that what seems to be a conflict of just laws is never that in fact. The truth is that many of these laws are *Lex Vulgus*, imposed by force rather than by a sense of what is just. As the manuscript is missing from this point on, we have no way of knowing what would have followed. It would have been interesting to know whether Cicero would have developed a method of distinguishing between laws. As it is, all we have is a taking up of the argument and its further elaboration by Lactantius.

Lactantius suggests that the difference between legal codes may best be accounted for by utility, in the sense of human prudence. St. Paul, I fear, would have termed this the specious virtue of human wisdom, which might be expressed in slang as a smart-alec sharp practice. There can be cases, observes Lactantius, in the vein of so many thinkers before him, when to follow justice would be the height of folly. Huntingdon Cairns in his excellent *Legal Philosophy from Plato to Hegel* has unfolded the argument that then follows very skilfully. Rome would not have won her empire and would have remained a poverty-stricken village if she had so great a care for justice as to forget utility. Respect for the provisions of the *Law of Nations* are not always conducive to victory in war. Prudence—utility—urges us to increase our resources, to extend our boundaries, become rich and the like. Justice inevitably limits these possibilities. Lactantius gives a number of examples of action that is just but by no means "smart". Declaring its faults before selling a runaway horse is one. Another is declaring the truth when buying gold from a man who believes it to be copper. Still others are not seizing the horse of a wounded soldier so as to flee a lost battle or not pushing a weak man off a plank that one finds after shipwreck.

It is striking to note that Lactantius failed to find a way whereby justice and utility could be combined in such actions. In today's language, he would seem to have had no time for situation ethics, which—under some forms at least—would strive to justify doubtful conduct in the name of prudential decision in the concrete situation. For some indeed "conscience" has become that which tries to unite justice and human prudence. Lactantius failed utterly to unite them, although he did make a couple of curious efforts in that direction. In the case of the shipwrecked man and the plank, he thought that the problem would not arise, for the truly just and prudent man—being content with his own land—will refrain from making a sea-voyage at all! And if, perchance, he should, heaven will surely protect him. As against the situationists, this latter kind of attitude reminds us of those contemporary conservative moralists who have little to offer the perturbed beyond an inculcation of patience and trust in God. If it is true to say that—particularly on the issues raised by *Humanae Vitae*—there has been a reliance by some people on conscience of a kind that seems to permit precisely what they want to do, it is equally true that others adopt a position whose logical implications are either that a man should not marry at all or, if he does, that he will not have the problems which perturb the former.

About one thing Lactantius was adamant—if it is at all possible that a conflict between justice and utility has to be faced, the just man will die rather than commit injustice. It would have been nice to know whether this would also have been Cicero's ultimate answer; it is as likely that it would have been as not. The meaning of it all is a firm belief in the superiority of the *Lex Coelestis* (and *Lex Naturae*) over the positive *Lex Vulgus*. Or to put it differently, a belief in the priority of fixed norms over a situationist type of morality based on a conscience that would put attention to circumstantial factors on a level with conformation to principle. We are therefore left with the stark possibility of conflict between what is morally right and what should be done to avoid folly. A choice has to be made between the two.

What a perennial problem this has proved to be. One choice is that of the tradition represented by Machiavelli, Hobbes and Nietzsche, who openly showed their contempt for morality and regarded justice as a quality of the weak. The other choice—was it also Cicero's?—has been that of Christianity, which upholds morality whatever the cost. The just may look foolish in the eyes of the world, but justice is simply not expediency. There is a third course—it was that of the Sophists—which seeks to escape the dilemma by *ex definitione* identifying justice and expediency. Sir Francis Bacon was an expert practitioner of the art of same, as when he persuaded James I that it was not only lawful but of moral obligation that he proceed with the expropriation and plantation of the land of Northern Ireland. The empire of Elizabeth I, no more than that of Rome, had not been extended by an over-scrupulous attention to the *Law of Nations*. The pirates Drake and Hawkins—founders of the Royal Navy —had little time for such scholarly asides. But their masters and mentors were ever ready to find factual considerations whereby their crimes were turned into patriotic achievements. Hypocrisy is the usual term that has been used to describe such fusing of expediency and justice. And in today's context, when the problem is as much a personal as a social one, one would fear greatly lest appeal to fact—analogous to that done by those mentioned above in the field of international law—is being used to "salve" consciences to the neglect of moral principle. But let us proceed with our historical reflections on the development of natural law.

4

The Universe of Thomas Aquinas

IT IS OFTEN said that a great thinker has to be so original in his world vision as to be entirely averse to every form of eclecticism. Strong thinking, it is suggested, must be so personal in character as to avoid all borrowing of ideas from others. Such opinions are fallacious, even if they die hard. It is undoubtedly true that many of the great philosophers of history—men like Aristotle, Hume, Kant, Marx—developed pivotal ideas which were exclusively their own and around which the rest of their intellectual edifices were constructed. But, on reflection, it emerges that what each of them achieved was to grasp a particular facet of reality. Otherwise it is hard to see how minds so great could be so divergent in their comprehension of a univocal subject matter. It emerges too that their limitation consisted in each pushing his own vision to the virtual exclusion of those of the others. And it is along this path that exaggeration leads to error. Thomas Aquinas's thought was cast in a different mould;

of an exclusivist extremism he would have none. Indeed the very strength of his intellectualism consisted precisely in the degree of respect which he accorded to the views of those who had gone before him. The ideas of Plato, of Aristotle, the Stoics and the Fathers of the Church, the ideas too of the Moorish thinkers and the early Scholastics, all found a place in his system. So much so, that to a great extent this system was one of syncretism and a powerful system not only for all that but because of it.

This is clearly evident in Aquinas's thinking on law and justice. He gives us two distinct definitions of law, deriving respectively from different ideological backgrounds. In the *Summa Theologica* (*1a 2ae*, Q.90, art. 4,c.) we read that "law is a promulgated ordination of reason for the common good by one who has care of the community". Several elements in this definition deserve notice; they show how Aquinas managed to combine ideas of different ancestry. First of all, law is an ordination of reason. Aquinas thus takes his stand firmly on the rationalist side, the main-stream of the western intellectual tradition. Not for him is the Sophist notion of law as something arbitrary, the product of chance, of mere convention. Its essence pertains to reason rather than will. Secondly, law is directed to the service of the common good rather than immediately and directly to the good of the individual. Here one discerns the ancient social dimension of law and justice, in the stream of the Aristotelian *polis* and the *cosmopolis* of the Stoics. The good of the individual is attained in and through the common good. Finally, law is something which proceeds from him who has care of the community.

Here I am persuaded that Aquinas intended to assign due role to the community itself in the fashioning of law. The modern idea of law as something made by the ruler is one that he would never have subscribed to. He did not have to insist that it is something which the ruler declares rather than enacts, for nobody at the time would have dreamed otherwise. A proper understanding of medieval thought on law and justice demands a considerable feat of mental gymnastics on the part of modern man. By and large, the nation States of later times had not emerged; the social fabric was a criss-cross pattern of interlocking feudal loyalties within which all members of the community had rights and duties. If the serf and the freeman had obligations to their overlord, he too had correlative duties towards them. In particular the ruler of substance —the prince or king—had the duty to ensure the customs and traditions of his people, the conspectus of rights which guaranteed their liberties. Law was the body of decisions whereby he did this against the ever-changing backdrop of life. All this is reflected admirably in the sentiments of the people, as expressed, for example, through their elected representatives in the coronation formula of the kings of Aragon: "We, the Cortes, who are as good as you, swear to you, who are no better than we, to accept you as our king and sovereign lord, provided you respect our liberties and laws, but if not we do not". This kind of thing was normal practice in the days of Aquinas, making it unnecessary for him to stress the fact that the community played an essential role in the fashioning of law. The ruler did not make law by reason as out of his own head alone. He had to ensure that not only was it geared to meet the needs of the community but as far as possible, stem from the community's own consciousness of its "felt needs"—he really declared law rather than made it.

In the *Summa Contra Gentiles* we get another definition of law, which at first sight seems quite different from that of the *Summa Theologica*. Law is now defined as a device for securing the ordination of man to his last end. Just as in the irrational creatures there is a complex of instincts which ensure that they achieve their purpose in being, so also man must have something to guide him in his free acts, "and this", says Aquinas, "we call law".

Note carefully that he is speaking of law *simpliciter*. There can be no doubt but that he intended the definition to apply to all law, whether of God, the State or the Church, indeed to all social prescriptions that take the form of law in any and every society. The amazing thing about Aquinas's maturer works—multiple and voluminous though they are—is how they hang together without confusion or contradiction. The definition of law of the *Summa Theologica,* on however different a plane it may be from that of the *Summa Contra Gentiles,* assuredly dovetails with this in the wider context of a whole-view of Aquinas's thought. To understand this it is even more necessary than I have stressed earlier to make a mental somersault from the concepts of our own day to those of Aquinas. If it be true to say that owing to the time-conditioned character of human categories it is well-nigh impossible to write about the history of events with complete accuracy, it is even more true when there is question of the history of ideas. Who would have thought today, for example, that when Aquinas spoke of the "common good", he was speaking not only of the good of the State but of the universe? Yet this is exactly the position. On more than one occasion he described God as the common good of the universe and of all its parts.

Against this background one begins to perceive that all law is basically one—that which conduces to the last end or common good. And even if the definition of the *Summa Theologica* may have had its proximate origin in a consideration of the law of the State, such as this was to be found at the time, it is equally applicable to all laws because all have the same purpose, the directing of man to his final end. The Aristotelian dilemma of the good citizen and good man failing sometimes to be happy is adroitly avoided in the Thomistic perspectives. Virtue and happiness stemming from human law is not everything; man's last end is to be found elsewhere. "The ultimate end of human life", wrote Aquinas in one passage, "is not to live virtuously, but by living virtuously to arrive at the fruition of the divine" (*De Reg. Princ., Bk.* I, c.14). One does this, but only partially, by being a good citizen. One also does it in a variety of other contexts, at the natural and supernatural levels. In each of them one is directed by law, a partial realization of the one fundamental law, the Law of the universe as such.

It would be a pity to pass from this without drawing attention to the way in which it incorporated yet perfected the ideas of law of both Aristotle and the Stoics. Those of Aristotle were framed in the context of the *polis,* the City-State, or what might be termed a *microcosmos.* Within this, law—in its essence—was a human thing, with no theological overtones whatsoever. The ideas of the Stoics, for their part, were framed in the context of the *cosmopolis,* the World-State, or what might be termed a *cosmos.* Within this, law—in its essence—was both human and divine, along the pantheistic lines proper to the Stoa. The ideas of Aquinas were framed in the still broader context of the Universe as a whole or what might be termed a *macrocosmos.* Within this, law—in its essence —was divine. But it was viewed as being participated in by God's creatures in different ways and to different degrees.

In the *Summa Theologica, 1a 2ae,* Q.72, art. 4, Aquinas sums this up as follows:

> There should be a threefold order in man. One order is that which stems from the divine law, by which man should be directed in all things. Another stems from the rule of reason, by which all our actions and passions should be regulated. And if

man were by nature a solitary animal, this twofold order would suffice. But because man is by nature a political and social animal, as is proved in *I Politic.* cap. 2, it is necessary that there be a third order by which man is ordered in relation to other men with whom he must live.

This threefold order is viewed by Aquinas after the manner of Chinese spheres, a series of three concentric circles. For he goes on:

Of these orders the first contains the second and exceeds it. For whatever is contained under the order of reason is contained under the order of God . . . . Similarly, the second order includes the third and exceeds it, for in all things in which we are ordered to other men we should be regulated by the rule of reason . . . .

These passages offer possibilities for abundant commentary, especially by way of comparison and contrast with the ideas of Aristotle and the Stoics. The divine law by which, as Aquinas describes it, "man should be directed in all things", is a kind of abstract and up-in-the-air idea of law. It connotes no particular concrete content. In this, as a concept, it resembles the "absolute justice" of Aristotle and the *"Lex Coelestis"* of Cicero and the Stoics. Then there is the reference to man being "a political and social animal", a concept which Aquinas says he derived from Aristotle. It is significant, however, that whereas Aristotle had spoken of man only as a "political" animal, Aquinas speaks of him as a "political and social" animal. Here we have a good example of the way in which he frequently corrected Aristotle, bringing his thought in harmony with Christian perspectives. Man as a political animal alone was an idea repugnant to

Christianity by reason of the totalitarian implications contained therein. Finally, the passage is indicative of the theist rather than pantheist persuasions of Aquinas in contradistinction to those of the Stoics. The order of reason—or the Natural Law—is under the order of God —or the Eternal Law—which exceeds it, as does the container the thing contained.

All this is developed further in the *1a 2ae*, Q.91, articles 1 and 2:

> Supposing the world to be governed by Providence . . . . it is clear that the whole community of the universe is governed by the divine reason. This rational guidance of created things on the part of God . . . . we can call the Eternal Law.
>
> (Now) since all things which are subject to divine Providence are measured and regulated to the Eternal Law . . . . it is clear that all things participate to some degree in the Eternal Law, in so far as they derive from it certain inclinations to those actions and aims which are proper to them.
>
> But, of all others, rational creatures are subject to divine Providence in a special way; being themselves *made participators in Providence itself*, in that they control their own actions and the actions of others. So they have *a certain share in the divine reason itself*, deriving therefrom a natural inclination to such actions and ends as are fitting. This participation in the Eternal Law by rational creatures is called the Natural Law . . . . As though the light of natural reason, by which we discern good from evil, and which is the Natural Law, were nothing else than *the impression of the divine light in us*. So it is clear that the Natural Law is nothing else than the participation of the Eternal Law in rational creatures.

Once again one is lost in admiration for the selective and constructive electicism of Aquinas. From the very outset the argument is conducted on the assumption that the universe is not fortuitous; providence not chance is its mainspring. A rational providence at that and not simply a voluntarist divine *fiat*. In fact, what is called the Eternal Law is really the rational plan of God for the behaviour of all his creatures. Elsewhere this primal law is defined by Aquinas as the plan of divine reason directive of all acts and motions. As far as the inanimate and the irrational creation is concerned, this plan is effected by means of physical and biological laws. No option to defect from it is open. With man the case is entirely different, for man is a creature of reason and free will. This is the cause of his dignity; it is also his frightening responsibility. For man, as Aquinas puts it, is made a participator in Providence itself. He is in fact the instrumental cause whereby the creator fashions his plan for man himself. An instrumental cause of a most un-usual kind, being the source of decision both in respect of the shape which the plan takes and of the extent to which he will subsequently observe it. In a sense, there-fore, man enjoys "a certain share in the divine reason itself". Stoicism? Yes and no. "Yes" in its linking of the natural law to the reason which guides the universe; "no" in its firm insistence that, despite this, man's reason is not God's.

Notice the phrase "a certain share". Whenever Aquinas was not quite sure of the exact nature of a situation, he always tended to employ qualifications like *quasi*. Here, when he says a "certain share", we ourselves can be cer-tain that he was not at all certain of the nature of the share in question. But it was definitely not Stoicism *pur sang*. The repeated reference to rational "creatures" shows this. And, at the end of the passage, where the light of reason is likened to "the impression of the divine light" in man, one feels that Aquinas is making a gesture in the direction of the theory of divine illumination by which St. Augustine had sought to explain the workings of reason. One feels too that, in doing this, he is intentionally leaving the door open to the illumination of man's natural reason by grace. In the Christian tradition of natural law—written about so well by Fuchs in his book on the subject (*Natural Law*, Dublin, 1965)—divine grace cooperates with reason in arriving at an understanding of what is right for man. Right for man, that is, on the level of the supernatural, which perfects but does not destroy what is natural. We may be sure too that the community dimension, which—as we have seen—Aquinas, like all the others takes for granted as an essential aspect of law, is open to including the contribution of the teaching Church in the understanding of natural law, guided by the light of grace in its individual members and appointed authorities. In this connection Fuch's last chapter on the importance of a Christian sociology is anything but out of line with Thomistic thought. For the Christian, the teaching Church is of inescapable relevance for the interpretation of the natural law. So much so, that it is possible to envisage a situation in which the humblest Christian, guided by the Church's insights, could be in possession of a higher grasp of the natural law than would the most sophisticated pagan on the purely secular plane.

Let us return, however, to the natural order unenlightened by grace. Perhaps the most notable single element in Aquinas's exposition of this, which has been practically forgotten today, is that man in truth *makes* the natural law. As law it is the law of reason, of man's reason—something rationally decided and freely followed. It is therefore made by man but under God. God, as it were, has sub-delegated or devoluted its elaboration to man. But it is an elaboration by way of rational construction out of materials supplied rather than of rational construction entirely *de novo*. To ignore the materials—his human make-up—would be to deliver only a pseudo natural law.

From one point of view, therefore, man makes the natural law; from another point of view he does not. Perhaps the best way to explain this is by way of drawing an analogy with the concept of human liberty in Marx. Popular expositions of Marxism describe it as a determinism in which man is not free to make his own history. But whatever about the position adopted by post-Marxian Marxists, this is not a faithful reproduction of Marx's own thought. For him man is definitely free but he exercises that freedom within certain restraints. As Marx put it: "Man makes his own history, but he does not do so out of conditions chosen by himself". For Marx the shape of historical epochs is determined not by man, but by the interplay of economic forces which it was Marx's special contribution to perceive, and which he carried to absurd extremes. Within this basic determinism, man is free to shape his everyday life.

In somewhat the same way, for Aquinas man makes the natural law, but he does not make it out of conditions chosen by himself. There is a vast difference between saying that man's history is completely freely-fashioned and saying that it is completely determined by forces outside his control. Likewise, there is a vast difference between saying that man exclusively decides on morality and saying that morality is something handed to him on a plate. The Stoics might be said to have had the latter view, seeing in morality, as in all things human, the inevitability of fate. But the contemporary situationists are saying something often not unlike the view that the individual man is absolutely free to construct morality for himself—albeit rationally—as seems best from situation to situation. He is in no way constricted by overriding general norms of a kind that are not geared to situations. The view of Aquinas represents an in-between that is in complete harmony with humanist aspirations. How unfortunate that a man like Sartre, in his *Existentialism is a Humanism* (Paris, 1946), should betray such ignorance of the true tradition of natural law.

The real difficulty about natural law lies less in the general establishment of its existence than in the setting out, even in broad outline, of its content. And yet the two are conected in that, unless the latter is done properly, it is not surprising if people tend to reject the former. On the question of content, Aquinas introduces some really important basic concepts that had their origin in the thought of Aristotle. I refer to his distinction between the principles of the speculative and the practical reason, so like Aristotle's distinction between theoretical and practical science. For Aquinas, in both speculative and practical knowledge, conclusions are reached by way of linking first principles and facts. First principles themselves are unproved and unprovable. Indeed they are not entirely different from what Kant was later to speak of as the categories of the speculative and practical reason. For him the principle of causality was a *datum* of the speculative reason, a presupposition without which speculation could not even begin. That of duty played a similar role in the practical reason, in that all thought concerning morality must begin with it. In the case of Aquinas, the first principles of speculative thought were those of identity and contradiction, and the correlative principle of excluded middle. Until Hegel, at least, the principle of identity—A is A—seemed undeniable; it is so basic than any attempt to prove it must assume it. In the practical order of moral behaviour Aquinas regarded as equally basic the principle "Good is to be done and evil avoided".

In both the speculative and practical domains the further one gets away from first principles, the more difficult it is to achieve certitude in knowledge. One can be immediately certain, for example, that a horse is a horse and not a motor car, because of the close connection of that assertion with the principles of identity and contradiction. It is quite other with an assertion that is remote from them, such as that dreams are sex fulfilments, in that it is not easy to see how a denial of this involves one also in a denial of one or other first principle. It is the same with affairs of the practical order, such as the statement that the just wage for a particular kind of work should be so many pounds and new pence. The more detailed one tries to be in a matter like that, the further one finds oneself from the principle that good is to be done. Or rather should I say that the further one descends into details, the harder it is to see how a denial of the statement involves one in a denial of this principle.

It will be appreciated at once how different is this Thomistic approach to knowledge from the positivistic model which was ushered in by the modern era of physical science. We shall have much to say later concerning this and concerning the Comtean thesis that the only valid knowledge is empirical. Dominated by the performance of a science that depended for its efficiency on exact measurements, men easily came to believe that only such data are at all valid. The results, as we shall see, were disastrous. Neither Aristotle nor Aquinas were so foolish as to fall for the view that all knowledge must be equally precise and certain. Knowledge of practical matters, of actions or becoming, simply cannot be on the model of the speculative knowledge of being.

Aquinas expands on the whole business at length in a remarkable passage in the *1a 2ae*, Q.94, article 4:

There is a difference between theoretic and practical reason. Theoretic reason is concerned with what is necessary, with what cannot be otherwise: truth is discovered in its special conclusions without exceptions, as it is also in its general principles. But practical reason, being concerned with human conduct, has to do with the contingent. And so, though there is a certain necessity about its general principles, the further it descends into detail, the more it may encounter exceptions. Thus in the theoretic order, there is the same truth for everyone, though it may not be equally recognised by all except in its very general principles. But in the practical order there is not the same truth or practical rightness for everybody, as far as detail is concerned, but only in general principles (and even in those for whom there is the same rightness it may *not be equally recognised by all*) . . . . . [For example.] It is right for all to act according to reason. And from this it follows in detail that things borrowed should be returned to their owner. This is right for the most part (*ut in pluribus*), but it *can in some cases be harmful,* and so against reason, as for example if what is returned comes to be used treasonably . . . . . And the further one descends into details, the more does this happen. Thus the natural law in its first more general principles is the same for all both as to what is right and in their recognition of it. But in relation to details which come as conclusions from these general principles, it is the same for all for the most part (both as to what is right and in their knowledge of it), but may, in some cases admit of exception as to what is right because of particular circumstances as well as not being known to all.

In other words, the natural law is not something absolutely immutable, a rigid and universal rule, equally clear and certain to all men. On the contrary, it is of its substance a somewhat flexible rule, of which the more general principles are the same and equally clear to all, but of which the particular principles can vary—within a respect for the general—and are also sometimes unknown to men. In one place Aquinas goes so far as to say that human nature is subject to change. What he means is that man is not just flesh and bones, that the culture which he fashions is part of himself, the environment which is necessary to his very existence. This is the same as saying that it is men rather than *man* that exist, with one culture in one place and another elsewhere—all of which is part of them as men. And while the natural law in its basic first principles is the same for all, it is open to change in its more concrete precepts.

These latter are really applications by way of the conjoining of first principles with the facts of experience. Thus secondary principles are conclusions drawn from the primary and themselves can be associated with further experience for the derivation of tertiary principles. The process of application is therefore neither a pure *a priori* rationalistic deduction—a drawing out of the implications of the essence of "man"—nor a pure *a posteriori* empirical induction—a classification and analysis of different situations. It is a combination of empiricism and rationalism—a teasing out of the meaning of the basic inclinations of man in his ever-changing historical existence. In all this matter Aquinas, if anything, is much more an existentialist than an essentialist.

Natural law, as he saw it, is adaptable; it can change both by way of addition and of subtraction. An example of addition is when new institutions become necessary in view of the development of human activities. The encyclical *Pacem in Terris* provides a concrete instance when it speaks of the need for definite machinery for the preservation of peace between States. At the present day a body like the United Nations has become so necessary that one could speak of it as being demanded by natural law. For, obviously, this is the case in respect of any institution on which international order today closely depends. Time was when even bloody conflicts in one part of the world were unknown to, much less disturbed, any other. Today the position is drastically different. And with the instruments of destruction currently at man's disposal, there is always a danger that a local war will escalate to the point of a holocaust that could consume humanity. In these circumstances, the fostering of international order becomes a moral imperative, a duty on men stemming from natural law. It is a duty of a kind that did not exist in earlier days, representing an important addition to the natural law.

There are also examples of how natural law can undergo subtraction. The changes which have taken place concerning the institution of slavery or the place of women in society are such. In early Christian times slavery was accepted by all as a natural and even necessary institution. Gradually, as a more developed Christian culture emerged, it rendered slavery incompatible with the dignity of man in a way that caused the institution to cease being acceptable in natural law. The same happened in the matter of the inequality of women and a variety of institutions attaching thereto. At the moment the big question which exercises moralists is whether demographic changes are taking place to such a degree as to justify the dropping of the prohibition of artificial contraception as a natural law precept at least for non-Catholics in certain circumstances.

It will have been noted that, in the last couple of paragraphs, I have spoken of natural law as both "institutions" and "precepts". The fact is that it does involve both. On the one hand, it consists of a body of directives or precepts by which the morality of the individual is determined. On the other hand, it is a series of institutions which are created and protected by civil law. Not

that the two coincide at every point; morality and legality
are not identical. What I mean is that, to a considerable
degree, the body of moral precepts, made up of the
secondary and tertiary principles of the natural law, are
related to the institutions which are enforced by civil law
and which in turn constitute the *Law of Nations*.

Indeed one of the most prominent features of medieval
thinking in this regard was the subordination of all human
law to natural law. Natural law was looked upon as the
foundation and ultimate criterion of the validity of civil
law. In the *1a 2ae*, Q.95, art. 2, Aquinas wrote as follows:

> St. Augustine says: "There is no law unless it be
> just". So the validity of law depends upon its justice.
> But in human affairs a thing is said to be just when
> it accords aright with the rule of reason: and, as
> we have already seen, the first rule of reason is the
> Natural Law. Thus all humanly enacted laws are in
> accord with reason to the extent that they derive
> from the Natural Law. And if a human law is at
> variance in any particular with the Natural Law, it
> is no longer legal, but rather a corruption of law
> (*non est lex sed legis corruptio*).

Commenting on this, in his treatise entitled *The
Natural Law* (London, 1951) A. P. d'Entrèves says:

> This is no academic statement devoid of any prac-
> tical significance. The words must be taken literally.
> They mean that allegiance to the State—even though
> it be the highest embodiment of natural morality—
> can only be conditional. Unjust laws are not properly
> laws. They do not, in consequence, oblige in con-
> science (p. 43).

What a contrast with Aristotle—and later with Hegel!

For Aristotle, as we have seen, the law of the State *was* the natural law; hence his problem about how to secure equity in cases where the law as it stood was inadequate. It was a problem to which he found no solution, due to his persistent refusal to attribute the ability to the man in the street to make up his own mind, that is, form his conscience as to what to do. Conscience, in fact, did not figure at all in Aristotle, nor, as a result, the notion of conscientious objection to law. The same was to be true later of Hegel, for similar yet different reasons. For him also the law of the State constituted morality for the individual; there could be no question of the law being unjust, nor room for the intervention of a conscience that had any function other than to reflect it.

As against these positions, the tradition of Aquinas and medieval Christianity attributed a prominent place to the promptings of conscience. This is to be seen both in its building in of the principle of equity into the very structure of natural law and in its insistence that unjust human laws do not bind in conscience. It would be amusing, if the matter were not such a serious one, to think that a principle to which so much importance was attached in the tradition of medieval Christendom, is being put forward today as if it were a new discovery of which previously the Church was in ignorance. The same is true of a number of other important principles, although it is also true that they are better understood today than formerly. Such, for example, is the principle that "Outside the Church there is no salvation". This was never understood officially as being absolutely exclusive and one remembers that it is not so long ago—yet during the pre-Conciliar period—when Father Feeney of Boston got into trouble for saying that it was. What is better realized now is that the number of the saved outside the Church is much larger than was once conceivable. Another such principle is that of religious liberty, which, to my knowledge, was never formally denied by orthodox Catholic teaching. Yet one gets the impression from the writings of Courtney Murray and others that it is something which has been discovered only recently. The most that can rightly be said is that, while admitted in theory, it found little practical application until recent times. Yet another principle with a similar history is that moral responsibility can be destroyed by the pressure of ignorance, concupiscence, fear and violence. Aquinas and his contemporaries were quite ready to admit this, just as contemporary psychiatrists do so in respect of the influence of temperament, cultural environment and conditioned reflexes. But whereas the latter take for granted a far-reaching and more or less constant impact on the part of these factors, the medievals seemed to believe that the reduction of freedom by irrational forces was an exceptional and unpredictable occurrence. The principle was the same, the emphasis different. So also with the principle of conscience. While undoubtedly there is a fuller understanding at the present time of its nature and the extent of its role, the principle itself has been granted for quite a while. It was in virtue of it that Aquinas held that unjust human laws—i.e. those laws which run counter to the natural law—are really not laws at all and do not bind in conscience. Of course the difficulty remains of knowing when this is so; the presumption will be in favour of authority. But the principle in itself is clear.

It was the medieval view that all law for human communities must derive from and reflect the basic law of the universe. It is hard for us today, when law is primarily understood as human law, to comprehend exactly this medieval way of looking at things. Strangely enough, despite the fact that the medieval period was one of the glorious periods of Christendom, even Catholic scholarship has somewhat neglected many aspects of it. More

6

weight has been attached to classical studies as an aid to patrology. For an appreciation of the politico-legal background that we are concerned with, much benefit could be derived from a perusal of books like *Feudal Society* by Marc Bloch (London, 1961) or of Sir Arthur Bryant's more recent *Medieval Society* (London, 1967). Gierke, in his classical work *Political Theories of the Middle Age* (Cambridge, 1900), has the following to say about the unity of law in medieval times:

> Every ordering of a human community must appear as a component part of the ordering of the world which exists because God exists, and every earthly group must appear as an organic member of that *Civitas Dei,* that God-State, which comprehends the heavens and the earth . . . . since the world is one organism, animated by one Spirit, fashioned by one Ordinance, the self-same principles that appear in the structure of the world will appear once more in the structure of its every part. Therefore every being in so far as it is a whole, is a diminished copy of the world; it is a *microcosmus* or *minor mundus* in which the *macrocosmus* is mirrored. In the fullest sense this is true of every human community and of human society in general. Thus the theory of Human Society must accept the divinely-created organisation of the universe as a prototype of the first principles which govern the construction of human communities (pp.7-8).

This meant that the human legislator—the king or prince as he was then—was regarded above all as the servant of the Law, who declared and determined it, rather than one who made law. It was a concept which today, within the Church at least, is being revitalized by the concept of hierarchy as service. The medieval dictum of Wippo put it well: *"Audiat rex quod praecipit lex; legem servare hoc est regnare"*. And an English source expressed the same thing as follows: "The Law is the highest inheritance of the king by which he and all his subjects are to be ruled, and if there were no Law there would be no king and no inheritance". The inheritance consisted of the liberties and customs of the people, the fruit of men's reason from time immemorial, enshrined (in the case of England) in the Common Law of the realm which, as far as jurisprudence went, represented the natural law. It was properly argued that if any measure or decision was once reasonable, it continued to be so if circumstances were unaltered. Hence justice as determined in the past must be handed down and continue to bind in the present. The Year Books of case law were its vehicle and the ruler who ignored them and the tradition which they represented was a tyrant against whom resistance could legitimately be offered.

Two Englishmen—one a cleric, the other a lay jurist—gave eloquent expression to these ideas. The cleric, John of Salisbury, did so in his *Polycraticus*, one of the finest examples of medieval literature on political theory:

> The prince obeys the law, the tyrant oppresses the people by rulership based on force . . . . . The will of the true ruler depends upon the Law of God . . . . but the will of the tyrant is the slave of his desire (*Bk. 8*, cc. 17 and 22).

And again:

> Who indeed in respect of public matters can speak of the will of the prince at all, since therein he may not lawfully have any will of his own, apart from that which law or equity enjoins (*Bk. 4*, c. 1).

Bracton wrote in similar vein (at the time of Aquinas):

The king ought not to be under man but under
God and then under the Law, because the Law makes
the King . . . . for there is no king where will rules,
not Law . . . . . As the servant and vicar of God
the king can do nothing on earth save that which he
may lawfully do. It is no answer to say that "What
the king wills has the force of law", for . . . . not
everything that the will of the king rashly conceives
. . . . has the force of law . . . . . As long as he
administers justice, he is the vicar of the eternal
king . . . . . A king is king when he governs well, but
a tyrant when he oppresses the people with violence.

The idea of the king as one who administers justice
recalls the medieval corps of *justiciers,* who functioned
for the king in the matter as his burden grew. So too does
the very term royal "court", originally a movable institution as the king did the rounds of his territory doing
justice. In fact the notion of legal justice as worked out
by Aquinas likened this virtue of the ruler to obedience.
Just as the subject was just by obeying the law so in an
analogous way was the ruler, in that his declaration of
what was just had to be in accordance with law. It is
true that he had to determine the law and interpret it in
the concrete, for which reason Aquinas termed his legal
justice "architectonic". It was an active and constructive
justice, yet nevertheless subject to law.

5

Absolutism and the Age of Reason

THE REFORMATION period was to set in train a chain of events and a line of thought which were to culminate eventually in an entirely new attitude towards natural law. In its final form this new attitude was to be known as positivism, which in essence was a total denial of the existence or relevance of natural law. In jurisprudence, legal positivism produced an idea of law as resting on foundations quite other than those of natural law, whether under the theological form in which it had been understood by either the Stoics or the Scholastics or under the purely human form of the more limited Aristotelian approach.

The end-term of this evolution was the emergence of an idea of law—civil law—as something more or less arbitrary in character, depending more on the will of the legislator than on a higher and universal rule of reason. Side by side with this deterioration in the tradition of natural law in jurisprudence, went a correlative deteriora-

75

tion of natural law in the field of individual morality. It will be interesting to see to what extent these developments were related and, in particular, to try to establish whether, in analogous ways, they were to lead ultimately to similar practical results.

Naturally, the growth of the new conceptions took time. It was a gradual process to which many factors contributed, some historical, some philosophical. In the domain of history the first changes came with Henry VIII's Act of Supremacy, by which he overturned not only the jurisdiction of the Roman Church in England but also injured the tradition of the Common Law. No such tradition was any longer to bind the king; the Year Books came to an abrupt and automatic end. Of which Burke was later to remark that "to put an end to the Reports is to put an end to the law of England". In other words, the Act of Supremacy had not only a theological significance but a profound relevance also for jurisprudence, in particular by its waiving of the Common Law and the natural law tradition contained therein.

Thomas More's refusal to accept the Act, while it was the stand of a faithful Catholic, was also in its intention and the language of its defence, the stout stand of a lawyer for the Rule of Law. Indicted for treason in 1535, his speech at the trial is memorable:

> For as this Indictment is grounded upon an Act of Parliament directly repugnant to the laws of God and His Holy Church, the supreme government of which, or any part thereof, may no temporal prince presume by any law to take upon him . . . . it is therefore in law among Christian men insufficient to charge any Christian man . . . . . For this realm being but one poor member and small part of the Church, might not make a particular law disagreeable with the general law of Christ's universal Catho-

lic Church, no more than the City of London being but one poor member in respect of the whole realm, might make a law against an Act of Parliament to bind the whole realm . . . . . And therefore am I not bound, my Lord, to conform my conscience to the councell of one Realm against the General Councell of Christendom.

More ended: "I die . . . . the King's good servant but God's first". His death marked the turn of an era. From then on—until recently—natural law was, as it were, on the run, both in the domain of jurisprudence and that of morality. By the time of James I the replacement of reason by will in human law, had advanced to quite a notable degree. Speaking in Parliament in 1609 the King said:

Kings are justly called Gods, for that they exercise a manner or resemblance of Divine power upon earth. For if you consider the attributes of God, you shall see how they agree in the person of a King. God hath power to create or destroy, make or unmake at his pleasure, to give life or send death, to judge all and to be judged or accountable to none . . . . . And the like power have Kings; they make or unmake their subjects: they have power of raising up or casting down, of life and of death . . . . accountable to none but God only.

What a contrast with the ideas of the earlier period, represented by the coronation formula of the Kings of Aragon! Accountability to the law—in the sense of the liberties and customs of the people—is now as dead as a dodo. In this respect the natural law has ceased to be relevant. But even though the king is no longer, to use Bracton's expression, "under the law", he still admits to being "under God". The atheism of the rationalist era is not yet upon us. The king accepts responsibility to God but not to Parliament. His law, he agrees, should be in accordance with the law of God, but only he himself is the judge of when it is so. For the king is not only a man but the anointed of God (cf. Kantorowich, *The King's Two Bodies*, Princeton, 1957) and in virtue of his charism as *vice Deus*, must be assumed to have an enlightened will. In some ways the argument is not unlike that which one hears today to the effect that the conscience of the Catholic should be his only guide to morality.

In a famous speech in the Star Chamber in 1616 James I set forth his position pretty clearly: "It is atheism and blasphemy to dispute what God can do . . . . so it is presumptuous . . . . in a subject to dispute what a King can do or say, that a King cannot do this or that: but rest in that which is the King's Will". Sir Edward Coke, who was present and who knew this to be against the tradition, at first ventured to express some qualifications: "Your Majesty, the law is the golden measure to try the cases of his subjects . . . . . The King cannot take any case out of his courts and give judgement upon it himself. The judgements are always given *per curiam* and the judges are sworn to execute justice according to the laws and customs of England". To which the King replied in a vein which shows how far removed he was from Bracton: "This means that I shall be under the law, which it is treason to affirm".

James I's argumentation was something like this. The basic fact is that I am the boss. True, I am not God, but I am God's anointed and representative on earth. In this capacity anything God can do, I can do. God can in fact do anything; therefore so can I. At this point Coke timidly reminded him of Bracton and of the medieval tradition of the natural law: "Sire, Bracton saith that the King ought to be . . . . under God and the Law". Whereupon, we are told, His Majesty "fell into that high indignation as the like was not known in him, looking and speaking fiercely with bended fist, offering to strike him; which the Lord Coke perceaving (*sic*) fell flat on all fower".

Truly, Sir Edward Coke was not made of the same stuff as was Sir Thomas More.

To these historical developments— and others like them on the Continent of Europe—were conjoined developments in political philosophy and the philosophy of law. In political philosophy the emergence of nation-States from the sixteenth century on, was linked with the emergence of an absolutist notion of sovereignty. It was a process to which both Catholic and Protestant writers contributed, depending on the masters whom they served. Already, in my *Studies in Political Morality* (Dublin and Chicago, 1962), I have outlined the role played by Albericus Gentilis and Sir Francis Bacon in moulding the views of James I in the sphere of politics. The resulting absolutism of his theory of the Divine Right of Kings found its most practical application in the nefarious Plantation of Ulster. But it was in France, in the person of Jean Bodin (1530–1576), that political absolutism found its best known apologist. It is in Bodin's *Republic,* which was written to defend the monarchial interests of Francis I against the ambitions of his greater vassals, that an "absolute and perpetual power" is assigned to the State. The growing, centralized and bureaucratic national State was now well on the way towards coming of age. In the seventeenth century its underlying philosophy was to be given succinct expression by Louis XIV in his well-known dictum *L'état c'est moi.*

Do not think for a minute, however, that there was as yet any developed philosophy of either political absolutism or legal positivism. All the writers of the period in question accepted without question that the king's will was limited by morality, that is, the law of God. What was new and most dangerous was the idea that the king's will really makes law and that he alone is the judge of whether it is just.

In the field of legal philosophy proper, this development was aided and abetted by the elaboration of what is called the voluntarist theory of law. In brief, this is the theory that the essence of law consists in a directive of will rather than an ordination of reason. It has had a long history in Christian thought, going back at least in rudimentary form, to St. Augustine. Its foundation was a certain suspicion of the ability of human nature to exercise reason in a way that is entirely reliable. St. Augustine's brush with Neo-Platonism and Manicheanism had done little to enhance his appreciation of human nature; neither, for that matter, had his personal experience as a young man. For which reasons, in his *City of God,* he had delivered himself of a number of utterances which have led many scholars to think that he did not believe in the natural and necessary character of the State. At the very least, the State for Augustine was something which was necessary only because of Original Sin—the product of a natural law for a fallen humanity, *pas grand' chose,* as the French would put it, and unreliable in its machinery of justice. For human reason, like human nature in general, has been profoundly disorientated by the Fall. Neither a natural law nor a human law which reflected it could guarantee justice and morality. St. Augustine felt that concrete proof of this abounded in the Roman Empire, the City of Man of his time.

Whatever may have been the exact import of St. Augustine's writing in this vein, after him a group of writers known as the Augustinian School came to develop them into a deep distrust of reason. But this was as nothing when compared with the downright deprecation of reason which came to be cultivated by Protestant theologians of the Puritan variety. In place of a natural law of reason these writers came to elaborate a doctrine of the absolute sovereignty of God (cf. their ideas on predestination), in accordance with which all law is grounded on the divine will, which can command or prohibit whatever it wishes. To find out what is just in private affairs —the sphere of individual morality—one simply and solely consulted the Bible. Here one notes the Protestant emphasis on Scripture and on its private interpretation at that. In the sphere of public affairs—of public morality —one discovered the will of God in the law of the State, which (by way of his own private judgement on the part of the ruler) was also expected to reflect the divine will of the Good Book. Nor was this something confined to the domain of theory. If d'Entrèves could write that the Thomistic principle of the right of conscience to refuse obedience to any unjust law, was an eminently practical principle and one that was actually acted on, so also was this Protestant belief that the will of the ruler should be accepted as the divine will for his subjects. In point of fact, since World War II, a number of German Lutheran theologians have ascribed the failure of German Protestants to mount resistance to Hitler's tyranny to this very ethical code.

The ideological developments of which we have been treating up to now in this chapter, were carried a step further in the political and legal philosophy of Hobbes (1588–1679). Hobbes too was a Puritan by faith. He believed strongly in a corrupt human nature, so corrupt indeed that it was a thing to fear and he has in fact been described as "a frightened Puritan". For him man's nature was but a complex of unruly passions; reason exists but is only enlightened self-interest. As against the animals, who are guided by irrational self-interest, man is a being of rational passion. But a being of passion just the same. As such, if he existed in a condition of nature, disorder and lawlessness would prevail to such a degree that life, as Hobbes put it picturesquely, would be "poor, nasty, brutish and short". It is for this reason that he needs society—the State in particular—whereby life may be made in any way tolerable. And so the State exists and men submit absolutely to its law. I don't think that there is any question of Hobbes believing that men ever got together historically and formally agreed upon the institution of political society. What he was saying really was that the State is not something essential to man, but that if it did not exist, unendurable chaos would ensue. Because of a realization of this, sparked by their rational self-interest, men are prepared to submit themselves to the rulership of men, endowed with the most complete coercive might. For government of these beings of passion and self-interest must necessarily be government by force. The ruler in fact must rule in such a way that order is maintained by creating a situation in which fear of breaking the law will be the greatest of all possible fears. Otherwise there would be the temptation to ignore the law and thus slip back into the unbearable state of nature.

Here one cannot avoid, for a moment, contrasting the teaching of Hobbes with that of John XXIII in the encyclical *Pacem in Terris*. For the former, order—peace —depends on force and fear, the very elements which *Pacem in Terris* brands as the foundation of a false peace, such as that which prevails today in the international order under armed force and the fear of nuclear warfare. In place of force and fear, it would substitute reason and love.

Hobbes combined political absolutism and voluntarism in law in the pages of his treatise on the State, the *Leviathan*. It was here that he delivered his definition: "Law in general . . . . is command". Not that he consistently denied the existence of natural law, as in some sense or another, the law of reason. It was too early yet for a clear break with natural law thinking. Hobbes of course believed in God and in a Providence directive of nature. Due to this, he could and did say that the ruler "is obliged by the Law of Nature and to render an account thereof to God, and to none but Him". The crunch point, however, is that, despite this, human law did not have to conform to natural law—however this might be conceived—in order to qualify for being accepted as valid law. In short, one finds in Hobbes an ironical and inconsistent version of what one might venture to call "a theological legal positivism".

In a number of places Hobbes himself gives evidence of being somewhat unhappy about speaking of natural law at all. And, on his terms, of course, well he might. Referring to the ideas concerning what is right—or human rights—which beings of rational self-interest conceive (and which for him was all that the natural law could possibly mean) he wrote: "These dictates of reason men used to call by the name of laws; but improperly: for they are but conclusions or theorms concerning what conduceth to the conservation and defence of themselves, whereas law, properly, is the word of him that by right hath command over others". What a contrast with the medieval position! Whereas then human law was accepted as law because it was like natural law, a thing of reason, for Hobbes natural law is not entitled to be called law because it is not like human law which is a thing of will. The primary analogate has switched places with the secondary. Whereas for the medieval tradition "law" connoted first and foremost the divine and natural law, from now on it will mean primarily the law of the State.

In short, for Hobbes, if the ruler is a competent and virtuous man, civil law will tend to coincide with the dictates of morality, but whether this be so or not, his law is to be regarded as valid law as long as he wills it—for this and for no other reason. It is not surprising, therefore, that Hobbes should say that, as far as jurisprudence is concerned, natural law was a *jus inutile*, a useless law.

It was largely in order to rectify this that the Dutchman Hugo Grotius (1583–1645) sought to reestablish natural law. Although himself a Protestant, he reacted strongly against the voluntarist concept of law, which had been the fruit of an extreme Puritan mode of thinking. He had good reason to know the extremes to which it could be pushed as Hobbes was one of his contemporaries. He set out, therefore, in his *De Jure Belli et Pacis* (1625) to put back the natural law as the law of reason. In view of the fact that the wars of religion were currently ravaging Europe, it was only to be expected that he should have sought to do so in the context of natural law insofar as this relates to international problems. He may also have remembered the fact that natural law had once been expounded in close identity with the *Law of Nations*.

Despite this, Grotius did not go back directly to the earlier pagan or medieval teaching on natural law. He tended rather to be guided by the Late Scholastic writers of whom Suarez was the most notable example. It is well-known that, even though it did have its own special merits, the Late Scholastic period was not the finest age of Catholic thought. While it did blaze new and interesting trails in some matters, it departed from the paths of the High Scholastic period on a number of important points. Nevertheless, in a sense, Grotius may be said to have continued the tradition of Aquinas, much as Hooker and the Caroline Divines did in England. However, by over-reacting against voluntarist ideas, he deflected just that little bit from the true tradition of natural law, with consequences that were eventually to be grave.

This deflection was less in the content than in the very basis of the natural law. While Grotius's definition of natural law was quite traditional, i.e. regarding it as that body of norms relating to conduct which man is able to discover by the use of his reason, he over-stated the case by arguing that these norms are valid in themselves quite independently of the fact that God has willed them. They stand up, as it were, in virtue of their inherent rationality. It is easy to make excuses for the overstatement; Grotius wished to defend the rationality of law. Still, in spite of the fact that the tradition prior to voluntarism had emphatically insisted that the essence of law lay in its being an ordination of reason rather than a directive of will, it was always realized that some element of will entered into it. As far as natural law was concerned, the will of God played a part when, as creator, He implemented his plan by way of the Divine Eternal Law. It is for this reason that the medievals had always seen the natural law as a participation in the divine *fiat* of the universe. It is because God made creatures as they are that the natural law for man is what it is. Hence, while the natural law was indeed conceived as the law of reason, it was never entirely divorced from the will of God. For Grotius it came to be so. He insisted that natural law would retain its validity even if God did not exist (*etiamsi daremus non esse Deum*).

To give him his due, this very assertion had already been made by some of the Late Scholastics. Suarez, who himself did not go along with them in it, had written of them as follows in his treatise on law: "These authors therefore seem lightly to admit that Natural Law does not proceed from God as a law-giver, for it is not dependent on God's will, nor does God manifest Himself in it as a sovereign commanding or forbidding". Indeed, he says, some of them go so far as to say that "even if God did not exist, or did not make use of His reason, or did not judge rightly of things, if there is in man such a dictate of right reason to guide him, it would have had the same nature of law as it now has" (*De Legibus*). It is quite likely that this was the source of Grotius's statement; his stance was by no means revolutionary. And yet there was all the difference in the world between the two formulations. The Late Scholastics who went in for this kind of thinking were fighting a voluntarism of an earlier kind and wished to stress the fact that natural law is something which lays down things that are intrinsically good or intrinsically bad, independently of the will of any sovereign, whether divine or human.

Grotius, of course, no more than these Late Scholastics, did not intend for a moment to actually deny the existence of God. He was advancing a purely hypothetical argument: "What we have been saying would have a degree of validity even if we should concede that which cannot be conceded without the utmost wickedness, that there is no God, or that the affairs of men are of no concern to Him". Grotius was neither an atheist nor a deist. But his approach did contribute quite substantially to the development of a purely rationalist conception of natural law. As somebody has so well put it, setting out to construct a system of law which would carry conviction in an age when theology was gradually losing its power to do so, he proceeded on the above hypothesis farther than anybody had done before. We must not forget that the era of rationalism had been ushered in and was now flourishing; Descartes had died in 1596. It was important for a natural law thinker, if his views were to gain acceptance, that he anchor them on foundations of human rationality rather than on what seemed less rational ideas about the will or even the reason of God, particularly as interpreted by any Church. To Grotius the Protestant, the role of the Church, as teacher of the natural law under the guidance of faith, was something that could only be described as repugnant. Equally so was the idea of law of any kind as reposing essentially on will. For Grotius, therefore, law was neither theological nor positive, but something which imposed itself by its inherent rationality.

On this basis he set out to construct a system of law quite independent of theological presuppositions. And what he started his successors continued, until what they stood for came to be accepted as the doctrine of a school. This secular, purely rationalist school of natural law was represented first and foremost by Pufendorf, whose *De Jure Naturae et Gentium* was published in 1672. Others were Burlamaqui, author of *Principes du Droit Naturel* (1747) and Vattel, author of *Droit des Gens ou Principes de la Loi Naturelle* (1758). The natural law, as developed by these writers, is a purely human rational construction. We are back again almost to the days of Aristotle, except that they do not refuse to pay homage more definitely than did he to some vague and remote notion of God. To a deity in fact—as became very evident in the pages of Jefferson and Condorcet—that was near to being exclusively a God of Reason. Did not the French Revolutionaries install the Goddess of Reason in Notre Dame? One thing anyhow is certain; the God of the eighteenth century rationalist philosophers was withdrawn from contact with or interest in men. Quite logically it followed that the Church might be ignored. d'Entrèves has put the matter well in his book on natural law: "The laws of Nature are to Jefferson the laws of Nature's God. The French legislators solemnly put themselves 'in the presence and under the auspices of the Supreme Being'. But Nature's God or the Supreme Being are not more akin to the God Omnipotent of the Creed than Deism is to Christianity" (pp. 52–53).

In other words, what Grotius had set forth as a hypothesis has now become a thesis for practical purposes.

7

It is now human reason rather than God—the Creator and source of the Eternal Law—that is at the centre of juridical philosophy. A human reason that is entirely autonomous, in that it is constitutive of what is unchangeably right and wrong. It is reason working in a vacuum, man making law out of his own head, rather than inventive in the sense of discovering what is there. How different from the Thomistic idea of a human reason that is not autonomous, that works on unveiling the meaning of a created reality, that takes due account of the facts of change, of history!

If this contrast seems too sharp, listen to what Grotius had to say about the necessary, abstract and clear notes of the natural law.

In the first place, it is endowed with a metaphysical necessity: "Measureless as is the power of God, nevertheless it can be said that there are certain things over which that power does not extend . . . . . Just as even God cannot cause that two times two should not make four, so He cannot cause that that, which is intrinsically evil, be not evil". Natural law is natural law whether God likes it or not, in somewhat the same way as for Leibnitz this is the best of all possible worlds, for God could do neither better nor worse.

In the second place, the natural law is abstract: "With all truthfulness I aver that, just as the mathematicians treat their figures as abstracted from bodies, so in treating law I have withdrawn my mind from every particular fact". What an extraordinary contrast with the Thomistic and even the Aristotelian position!

In the third place, natural law is something eminently clear to all who are endowed with reason and use it: "I have made it my concern to refer the proofs of things touching the law of nature to certain fundamental conceptions which are beyond question; so that no one can deny them without doing injustice to himself. For the principles of that law, if only you pay strict heed to them, are in themselves, manifest and clear, almost as evident as are those things which we perceive by the external senses".

Conceived along these lines there was little alternative but that natural law should become a system of inflexible rationalizations concerning the rights and duties of man. As it was, due possibly to the influence of Protestant individualism, due also, possibly, to the fact that this was in any case an age of individualism, the catalogue came to be presented mainly as one of natural rights and the natural law, understood as a vindication of the rights of the individual. It is at this time that we begin to hear so much about "The Rights of Man" and that the French and American Revolutions produced their Declarations of Rights. In short, natural law theory had become a theory of rights instead of what it used to be, a theory of law.

It is true that the phrase *Jus Naturale* continued to be used, but it was no longer the *Lex Naturalis* of earlier times. This is something the import of which has been neglected by John Courtney Murray and particularly in his book *We Hold These Truths* (New York, 1960). The fact that the basic socio-political principles of the American Republic derive from the natural rights tradition of the eighteenth century does not necessarily mean that in every respect they are to be presumed to be in harmony with the content of natural law. Prior to this, "right" and "law" were described by the same Latin term *jus*, which concealed the ambiguity and possible divergence. Hobbes in fact had noted this in his own time: "They that speak of this subject (are) used to confound *jus* and *lex*, right and law: yet they ought to be distinguished; because right consisteth in liberty to do, or to forbear, whereas law determineth, and bindeth to one of them: so that law and right differ as much as obligation and liberty". The

Roman jurists of old had known better. Distinguishing between a subjective and an objective *"jus"*, between a *facultas agendi* (or right to act) and a *norma agendi* (or rule of action), they saw a difference yet a relation between them in a way that Hobbes did not. The two were correlative, not antithetic. You can only have a *facultas agendi* (a right) because of the existence of a *norma agendi* (a law). One cannot exist without the other and, of the two, the notion of law is the more basic. But this was all before the eighteenth century or the doctrine of natural right which then emerged. For Wolff, whose division of philosophy is the supreme example of the cut and dried approach of the eighteenth century, the only meaning of *jus naturae* is that of "natural right": "Whenever we speak of natural law (*jus naturae*) we never intend the law of nature but rather the right which belongs to man on the strength of that law, that is naturally". Natural law has been finally transformed into a system of natural rights (freedom to act), apprehended primarily by the reason of the individual. Once again I have to ask myself whether there is not an analogy here between the development of an individualist idea of legality, centred on reason that is not law, and the contemporary emergence of a morality centred on conscience? We shall investigate the possibility further as we proceed.

6

The Separation of Legality and Morality

THE BEGINNINGS of the development, which was to culminate in the separation of legality and morality and the replacement of a system of values by pure positivism in both spheres, came with the rejection of the theory of natural law as a foundation to political and legal institutions. This, when one looks hard at it, shows itself to have been the inevitable counterpart of the deterioration of the system of natural law into one of natural rights. It found its first expression in what is known as contractualism or the theory that politico-legal institutions stem from a social contract between men. I am referring particularly to the philosophical views which appeared in Locke's *Treatise on Government* (1690) and which were developed and popularized by Rosseau and others. According to d'Entrèves, "the theory of the social contract would hardly have been possible had not the modern notion of natural law provided its basis" (p. 56). For, the accent now being on the individual and his rights, "the social contract was the only possible way left for deducing the existence of social and political institutions once the reason of man was made the ultimate standard of values".

What is meant really—and it does make sense—is that, once the reason of man had become the exclusive criterion (all reference to a "higher law" represented by tradition and the Church ruled out), the only way in which social and political institutions could come into being was by way of reasonable agreement between men. In this way a method could be found of providing the institutional system for the safeguarding of their rights. Legality—or public order—had become a matter of collective assent. Once again, one is tempted to speculate whether the substitution of individual assent—understood of course as reasonable—is an inevitable result of the current suppression of natural law by conscience as the basic criterion of individual morality? As far as the legal order went, the meaning of contractualism was the rational establishment by individuals of "a relationship of mutual obligation, which would not otherwise exist by the law of nature" (d'Entrèves, p. 57). One may well pose the question whether an ethic of responsibility that is centred on the dictates of the individual conscience may not be compelled to base self-obligation on a kind of private contract once the natural law has been removed? If living with others in political institutions demands agreement in such circumstances, the suggestion puts itself forward that, in similar circumstances, morality as solely a matter of conscience reduces itself to living peaceably with oneself.

Let us proceed first with a continued elucidation of the consequences of individualism in the sphere of legality. The first and most obvious was the appearance of a theory of relative natural rights according as the content of community contracts varied. This in fact was the message of Montesquieu's *Éspirit des Lois,* which appeared in 1748. As was usual at the time, Montesquieu held for natural law but in its current form of natural rights. He held too that the civil law of the State should take good care to respect these rights. But—and this was the original contribution of his work—he indicated clearly that there could be wide variations in the law in accordance with the different circumstances of history, climate, religion, and all those elements which create a different spirit between peoples.

It was only to be expected that this kind of relativity should emerge once the doctrine of the social contract was accepted. For this replaced fixed norms by agreed norms, at least in the sphere of politics and civil law. And, due to the intimate relation which had traditionally existed between legality and natural law, it was quite normal that the concept of agreement should inevitably slip over to being applied also to the natural law itself or, as it was now understood, to natural rights. The end term was a theory of flexible natural rights that, in more traditional language, would have been called a relative law of nature. Rights stem solely from the facts of given situations and in no way rest on fixed natural principles.

It may be said in defence of this that it had the considerable merit of reintroducing the consensus of the community in matters of natural law as that law was now understood. But there was a great difference between the role of the community in the determination of natural law as traditionally understood and that which was now accepted. Perhaps the best way in which this difference can be underlined is by following up the consequences of the contractual innovation.

Jean Jacques Rousseau, in the book from which the "social contract" got its name (1762), carried the theory to its logical extremes. He was aware that there was little point in making a distinction between "natural" and "civil" rights if in fact both had their origin in community agreement. It was quite possible, of course, that a tyrannical ruler could get into power who would impose a system of civil rights that did not at all accord with what the community regarded as right. In such circumstances there would be a broad abyss between civil and natural rights. But this kind of thing must be regarded as exceptional. The normal thing is for the community to govern itself, in which case civil and natural rights will coincide. For the social contract, which is at the basis of political living, ensures that democracy is the normal type of government.

For Rousseau the social contract, community agreement, democracy, means that whatever is done by the representatives of the people is right. Right, that is, both in the civil and natural senses. Indeed the distinction between these two begins increasingly to wane as Rousseau deepened the implications of his political philosophy. The law of the State, he said, necessarily reflects the "General Will" of the community, which is a kind of amalgam of the particular wills of the citizens insofar as each of them gives assent to the system of political institutions. As such, the will of the State is in some sense the will of each citizen and by this very fact whatever it does is willed by the citizens as a whole. The upshot of it all is that the law of the State must *ipso facto* be assumed to be expressive of natural rights. The general will of the community has become the only criterion of law, as long as it is really the general will. Government is unjust only when its laws are the will of a clique or a usurper. Rousseau knew full well how difficult it is to get unanimity or even a broad consensus from the whole community. And so he settled for the rule of the majority as sufficient to ensure respect for justice.

The "General Will" of the community can do no wrong. The common conscience, in other words, of the citizens can do no wrong. The will of the majority is always right. The government of the people is just. How often these phrases keep cropping up in the literature of liberal democracy. And, as a theory, the whole thing is attractive by reason of the place which it accords to the common consent of the community which, as previously outlined, has always been accepted as an important criterion of what is right. And yet we know also that the theory of liberal democracy did not save peoples from committing the greatest crimes. History has proved clearly that the "General Will" can make mistakes, that the people can certainly do wrong, that what is legally prescribed is not necessarily right. Entire volumes have been written in recent decades—but only in recent decades—to show that the theory of the "General Will" can and has ended up in Democratic Absolutism. The emergence of Hitler's Germany was the case in point which sparked off the realization that the theory is frankly false. Two books stand out in this connection, *The Heresy of Democracy* (London, 1954) by Lord Percy of Newcastle and J. L. Talmon's *The Origins of Totalitarian Democracy* (London, 1952).

We are not concerned here with the details of these developments. What does concern us is the way in which the abandonment of the natural law led to collective arbitrariness in government. Not that natural law or natural rights had as yet been formally abandoned as the basic criterion of civil legality. But this had become so closely identified with the will of the community that, for practical purposes, only what the community decided was of importance. The whittling away of the natural law as a higher rule of reason—in its basic principles above the community and under which the community has obligations—had produced a vacuum in which whatever the community decided must necessarily be legally right.

Here again one cannot fail to note the analogy with

the deterioration of natural law in matters of individual morality. Is not the will of the individual, operating in the vacuum left by the rejection of natural law, open to the same dangers as those which befell the will of the community? If the latter (i.e. the rule of democratic government) were to prove an unreliable guide in matters of legality, is it not likely that the former (i.e. the rule of the individual conscience) might prove equally unreliable in those of morality?

As yet, in the eighteenth century, this question could not be posed with clarity because the spheres of legality and morality were still related. Not at all identical or as closely related as they had been for the ancient and medieval worlds. But closely related for all that. While Rousseau now and then made a gesture in the direction of a sphere of natural law morality, which guided men in their conduct as private persons, as public persons he would have them take their morality from the State, from the legality which stemmed from human law.

It did not take long for a reaction against this to get under way. The idea that legality and morality must in any way necessarily coincide, while it might prove acceptable against the medieval perspective of law, was open to many objections under its new-found formulation. These were perceived with great perspicacity by Kant (1724–1804), who introduced the first formal separation between legality and morality. For Kant the sphere of legality is that of the accommodation *inter se* of the *external* liberty of men in community. It is the reasonable, practical, limitation of their freedom to do what they will as individuals in the context of living with others. Over against this, is the sphere of morality, which is the regulation *intra se* of the *internal* liberty of the *individual* man by way of the dictates of his private conscience. Just as law governs the actions of men together, so conscience—the manifestation of man's practical reason in his own regard—governs the actions which he is otherwise free to will in the external forum. And whereas legality can vary from community to community as attitudes towards what should be public norms vary, morality is a matter of the categorical imperative of the individual conscience, his own private sense of duty.

While frequently the demands of legality and morality may coincide, it is always something accidental rather than necessary. Legality is what is done under external constraint or sanction, morality what proceeds from a sense of duty or inner kind of constraint. Despite the constraint, Kant's objective in both cases was the preservation of liberty, on the one hand the liberty of men in community, which depends on some curtailment of their individual wills, on the other hand the liberty of the individual man, which equally depends on his placing some restraints on a will that can so easily be led by passion. Yet in spite of the laudable objective, the ironical outcome was a theoretical system which left the door wide open to legal repression and moral permissiveness. In the political sphere once all formal connection between legality and morality had been broken, the rights of the individual were no longer guaranteed as they had been in the past by natural law and could in theory be sacrificed to the demands of the common good as dictated by the autonomous conscience of the community. An arbitrariness had entered the field of legality that could all too easily terminate in erecting the State into an absolute. For, while it might in fact do so, it was not the purpose of legality to reflect morality. It was not in fact even bound to respect it. Similarly, in the sphere of morality, the disestablishment of natural law in favour of individual conscience was also conducive to an arbitrariness, but an arbitrariness in that morality entirely depended on conscience, which from another point of view erected conscience into an absolute.

The concrete results of this twofold process towards legal and moral absolutism were entirely different and hard to foresee. Whereas in the legal sphere it led to a system in which liberty came putatively to be defended by political repression, in the moral sphere it led to an autonomy of the individual conscience of a kind that made it hard to distinguish between liberty and licence.

A determined effort to reconcile these contradictions in both spheres was made by the philosophy of Hegel (1770–1831). It is not necessary for us here to go into the historical and metaphysical details relating to the emergence and content of his general system. It will be sufficient to recall its central points. These were, firstly, that reality is rational, that is, the stuff of which it is made is idea, the working out of the Divine Mind which encompasses it. Hegel, in other words was a pantheist, for whom reality was idea in the mind of God. Secondly, and immediately flowing from this, was the view that the key to the development of reality is logic. Obviously, if reality is something conceptual. Thirdly, for Hegel, logic or dialectic was a process of arriving at knowledge by means of a combining of contradictions. This was the clue to the understanding of reality, whether in its static or dynamic dimensions.

In the domain of politics and legality, as in all other domains, the same logic of contradictions holds good. Every concept is really the fruit of a fusion of opposites, every advance in meaning a carrying further of same. Along these lines concepts like those of the State and law must necessarily consist of a union of opposites. And so we find Hegel defining the State as an association which defends and protects with social force the interests of all, yet in which each, while subordinating himself to the good of the whole, at the same time pursues his own good. In the language of the dialectic, it is an idea which includes, and indeed reconciles within itself, both the claim of the community to the subordination of the individual and the simultaneous claim of the individual to freedom. The thesis is the domination of the community, the antithesis the liberty of the individual, the synthesis political society. This is the logical, the rational position and the rational is the real. As Hegel saw things, on the one hand the State ensures all legitimate human freedoms, while on the other hand it denies to the individual all right to challenge its authority.

It was possible for him to maintain this position only because of a more basic reconciliation of opposites, i.e. between the will of the community and that of the individual in a unified common consciousness that was creative being.

> "In considering freedom", he wrote, "the starting point must be, not individuality, the single consciousness, but only the essence of consciousness; for whether man knows it or not, this essence is externally realized as a self-subsistent power in which individuals are only moments".

The common consciousness of the community is the basic reality and the State is the high point of community. In these perspectives the consciousness of the State is given expression through its laws to which the consciousness of the individual, as a facet of that of the State, automatically gives assent. As Hegel put it: "The spirit of a nation controls and entirely dominates from within each person (so that) he feels it to be his own very being (and) looks upon it as his absolute final aim". From this viewpoint there could be no anomaly of the kind that Kantianism involved by way of political liberty coming to be ostensibly maintained by legal repression.

Nor, for that matter, was there room for the further Kantian anomaly of inner liberty turning into licence under the absolute direction of an autonomous moral conscience. In the Hegelian framework both the individual conscience and the common conscience of the community were each a welling-up of the one creative consciousness which equally constitutes the core of both. They were but different facets of the idea, which is Reality, the self-realizing existent Absolute Being.

It was all very metaphysical and rather remote from everyday life, but one requires little perception to see that it failed in its intent, namely, the construction of a philosophical system which could show how human liberty is compatible with legal and moral absolutism. On the contrary, in the domains of both legality and morality, the predominant factor was the law of the State—the will of God. Wrote Hegel: "It is absolutely essential that the constitution should not be regarded as something made, even though it has come into being in time. It must be treated rather as something existent in and by itself". It is an organic entity which expresses itself in its laws, from which the individual citizen takes his moral style of life. As the nineteenth century English Hegelian, Bosanquet, put it: "A man's life with its moral duties is, in the main, filled up by his station in that system of wholes which the State is, and . . . . this, partly by its laws and institutions, and still more by its spirit, gives him the life which he does live and ought to live".

Despite Hegel's protests, this resembles the ancient idea of the City-State, in which justice for the individual was determined by the pattern of law. In other words, morality and legality have again been fused in the law of the State. The only difference is that this is no longer a human law; it is the legal manifestation of the process of creative evolution, not even a pantheistic natural law of the Stoic variety but, as it were, their *Lex Coelestis* come down to earth. The domain of the absolute and eternal is in the here and now, and finds its highest expression in the working out of political life. The State, said Hegel, is a "self-knowing and self-actualizing" entity, "the march of God in the world" (*Philosophy of Right*, p. 279).

Hegel tried to show—vainly—that the legal and moral freedom of the individual can be achieved in fact only by subjection to the State. His thought on this followed a twofold pattern. First, as regards legality. Seeing that the will of the individual citizen is a facet of the transcendent will of the State, to follow this is necessarily to be free. Unlike Rousseau, who envisaged the possibility of a person willing something by a purely individual or private will, as against the institutional will whereby he acquiesced in community decisions, Hegel did not allow any form of purely individual volition which could conflict with the will of the State. Rather were there two sorts of freedom and in being utterly subject to the law of the State a man was exercising one or other form of it. On the one hand, there is the freedom which goes hand in hand with an obedience to the law that springs from inner conviction rather than from force or fear. This Hegel calls "subjective liberty". On the other hand, there is an obedience of fact, or material obedience, which is really external submission to the law. But let nobody think he is not free even if forced. For as the State is itself a rational entity, conformity to it, in so far as it is rational action, is free action, the expression of what Hegel called "objective liberty". Freedom, as rational volition, has thus been extended by Hegel to cover situations in which it can coexist with coercive legality.

There are points of similarity and of difference between this and the Scholastic concept of freedom. For the latter, individual liberty, whether in the sphere of legality or of morality, can be diminished and destroyed by the influence of non-rational factors. In conceiving freedom as something rational there is agreement with Hegel. The divergence of views arises in that whereas for the Scholastics these factors include ignorance, concupiscence, fear and violence of all kinds, for Hegel freedom simply cannot be destroyed by the kind of fear and violence represented by the force of the State. The State, now as God, elicits a new "freedom of the sons of God", so that no matter how absolute it may be in respect of legality, it is never so at the expense of individual liberty.

Secondly, as regards morality. Concentrating on the fact that true moral action always consists in acting in accordance with an inner moral will, and that anything else is either pretense or licence, Hegel marshalled a powerful argument to the effect that human liberty is not infringed by being subordinated to the State. In this again he was with the Scholastics in certain respects. For them too moral action is something that is triggered off by free volition; immorality is the fruit of the irrationalism of following passion; it is a kind of determinism rather than freedom. But they had no room for a determination of moral action by the State of a kind that could be said to be compatible with freedom. In his views on this Hegel may be said to have been influenced by Kant, and notably by his central thesis that moral action is that which is performed from an inner sense of duty, of a free response to the conscience or the moral will of the individual. *Be not forced from outside* was its motto. But Hegel differed from Kant in holding that the individual conscience is meaningless in isolation from the individual's relations with his fellow-men in community. In other words, the naked individual conscience is no guide apart from the common conscience of the State. It is the latter, especially through law, that proposes a life-style to the individual, a social righteousness within which he can be responsible in accordance with the dictates of his own conscience. Law is the instrument of the State by which, in the main, its pattern of right and wrong is enforced externally. But without law it would be impossible even to know what is right. The good life is therefore also dependent on the State, as it were, internally, that is, in the sphere of the individual conscience.

In short, the State is the beginning and the end of both legality and morality. It is the only source of the individual's rights and the source too of his duties. "The State", wrote Hegel, "is the ultimate end which has absolute rights against the individual". And Bradley, another of the English Hegelians declared: "The State is the guardian of our whole moral world". The consequences of this, both for legality and morality, are too well-known to call for repetition here. One needs little imagination to see the omnicompetent State around the corner. This in itself was repellant to many, more particularly in that Hegel all too easily spoke of the State as finding its perfect expression under the German form. There was also the fact that Hegelian metaphysics was difficult to understand, too difficult in fact to appeal to great numbers. Indeed ironically it was to find its widest use by Marx and his followers, whose thought in many respects would have been unacceptable to Hegel. The peculiar Hegelian reconciliation of absolute norms and human liberty never exactly became a dominant philosophy. There was too much idealism and pantheism involved in it for some. Others could not accept that morality and legality could be identical.

Thus failed the most notable attempt that was made to accept elements of Kantianism while avoiding its anomalies. The result of it all was that in theory and practice legality and morality again began to drift apart. From now on the history of the former is that of the emergence of legal positivism, of the latter the emergence of an ethic of the individual conscience.

8

7

Positivism in Law: Juridical Arbitrariness

IN 1902 the English jurist Sir John Salmond delivered himself of the following statement:

> The idea of a law of nature or natural law . . . . has played a notable part in the history of human thought in the realm of ethics, theology, politics and jurisprudence. It was long the accepted tradition of those sciences, but it has now fallen on evil days, and it can no longer be accepted as in harmony with modern thought on these matters.

Another writer around the same time echoed these sentiments, saying that natural law had gone on "the scrap-heap" of legal ideas.

It is this kind of thinking that laid the foundations for the emergence of legal positivism. Positivism in law might be described as the view that legality rests on some basis other than natural law. It is most generally expressed

104

under the form of what is called statist positivism, namely, that law stems from the naked command of the legislator as embodying the will of the State. It matters not whether the legislator be monarch or parliament, once a law has issued from whatever be the prescribed machinery, it is *ipso facto* valid law. This is the primary form of legal positivism and represents the correlative in legal philosophy of the modern political philosophy of absolute sovereignty.

Related to the primary form by way of an inadequate distinction are three further versions of legal positivism. The first—or nationalistic positivism—introduces a qualification into statist positivism by saying that the will of the State should reflect the spirit of the nation. It had its origin in the rise of the ultra-nationalist political philosophies which appeared in a number of European countries during the earlier decades of the twentieth century. Secondly, there is a communistic form of legal positivism, which stems directly from the influence of Marxist philosophy. As this sees things, law, as the command of the State, must reflect the interests of the dominant class. Finally, there is sociological positivism, which grew side by side with empirical sociology and which maintains stoutly that law, while it is essentially the command of the State, must always spring from the sociological situation and formulate the consensus of the community.

The classical exposition of statist positivism was that given by John Austin in 1861, in his famous *Lectures in Jurisprudence*. Law, he said, is "a rule laid down for the guidance of an intelligent being by an intelligent being having power over him". Notice the phrase "of an intelligent being". There is no question of law being based on physical force alone or of political life being a mere resultant of force. Gumplowicz's theory that human government emerges as does leadership in a herd of elephants is poles apart from what Austin represented.

For animals are not intelligent beings in the sense intended. Yet neither is his notion of law based on moral force. It is an instrument for the guidance of an intelligent being, it is true, but "by an intelligent being having power over him". This emphasis at this point is on force. Law, in other words, is not reason plus moral force but reason plus physical force. It is a doctrine of power rather than of authority. So the only basis of obedience is force, in that whatever directive can be forced on an intelligent being by another is entitled to be regarded as law. It leaves the door open for the kind of situation which Hobbes envisaged when he said "in matters of government, when nothing else is turned up, clubs are trumps". Yet it found influential confirmation in the legal texts of the late nineteenth century, which created the intellectual climate in the law schools well into the present. Sir Thomas Holland's *Elements of Jurisprudence*, which was first published in 1880, had gone into thirteen editions by 1924. It was entirely Austinian in its approach to law.

Despite the vogue of statist positivism as explained in such works, it quickly ran into a number of difficulties. The biggest and most obvious of these was that the theory left no room for any limitation of the power of the State. At least, it itself contained no built-in safeguards. The dangers to which it was open became alarmingly evident after Jhering in Germany had further developed it in his *Evolution of Law* and other volumes. "Law", he said, in *Der Zweck im Recht* "is the policy of force"; "Law is the aggregate of the coercive norms operative in the State". The same ideas were taken up and further elaborated by Köhler and in France by Ripert and de Malberg.

So frightening were these ideas that we soon find an effort being made to provide some way of ensuring a due limit to the power of the State. The most notable attempt to do this was that of the German jurist Jellinek in his well-known theory of the "Auto-Limitation of the State". For Jellinek the State by means of its constitution can furnish a self-built method of curbing its own legal power. It was a brave attempt to take the sting out of statist positivism by way of introducing into it a kind of built-in safeguard. But it quickly proved unsatisfactory on a number of counts. For one thing everything depends on how constitutions are interpreted. Unless guided in their decisions by a higher code, judicial decisions can stultify any constitution. For another thing what the State has given, it can equally take away and rights that are guaranteed only by a current consensus rest on a very fragile base indeed. How clear this has become in the context particularly of the United Nations Declaration of Human Rights. This contains those rights and those rights only on which the parties to it were prepared to agree. From the start there were difficulties like this involved in statist positivism, which theories such as those of Jellinek failed to remove.

There were other and important difficulties also— philosophical, historical and anthropological. Philosophers of law have been quick to point out that it allows for no real difference between a "must" and an "ought", between a coercive order and an obligatory order. That law pertains to the latter rather than to the former category has been particularly well underlined by H. L. Hart of Oxford in his logical analysis of the matter in *The Concept of Law* (Oxford, 1961). To this difficulty the historical school of law has added another, pointing out that law as it has developed over history runs counter to a simplistic statist positivism. Sir Henry Maine in his *Ancient Law* (1861) and Pollock and Maitland in their *History of English Law* (1898) had shown conclusively that a positivistic explanation of the crude statist kind leaves a great deal of law unaccounted for. It certainly is not applicable to ancient and medieval law, which was largely a fabric of custom and consent, something found rather than willed by the ruler. One has only to remember the dicta of John of Salisbury in medieval times to the effect that the legislator has in fact no will of his own. Lastly, the sociology of law has mounted a difficulty against a straight positivism on the basis of cultural data from primitive societies. Malinowski, in his *Crime and Custom in Savage Society* (London, 1926) has repudiated the theory on these grounds. He has shown that what moves such societies and introduces order within them is really the force of the mores of the community. In a cross-cultural perspective it quickly emerges that law, as conceived by the statists, is a rather sophisticated thing that is far from being known everywhere, whereas order—of the kind that in the higher societies stems from law—is ensured in many other societies by a wide variety of ways. These ways maintain legality without doubt but not in a way that harmonizes with statist positivism. To give but one example, in Eskimo society litigation can be settled by means of a juridical song contest between the parties. In certain other societies crime is punished by subjecting the victim to the laughter of the community.

A really determined effort to refine legal positivism was made by the German jurist Hans Kelsen. Kelsen was well aware of the kind of difficulties which we have catalogued, even if the documentation to back them was not as extensive in his time or as detailed as it is today. He set out therefore to work out a theory of law which would get over them while at the same time remain essentially positivistic. To this end he sought to construct a science of pure law, like to pure mathematics, which would rid law of all heterogeneous elements and would cover all its forms. As well as reducing law to its core and making it easier to identify within a variety of laws, the shedding of heterogeneity, such as nationalist overtones to law, could also be useful in eliminating one of the chief causes of the misuse of law by the State and thereby help to limit political power. But he was equally definite that all traces of morality must be removed from the factors which determine law. As a Kantian he regarded morality as a heterogeneous element in relation to law; to say that a law is just or unjust is to moralize; the jurist must confine himself to the law itself; otherwise a legal science is impossible.

Although a Kantian, Kelsen was interested in a different aspect of things from those in which Kant himself was interested. Whereas the latter sought to protect morality from the heterogeneous element of legality, the former sought to protect legality from that of morality. The result was the *"Pure Theory of Law"*. Avoiding the philosophical objections which can be laid at the door of ordinary statist positivism, Kelsen laid it down that law is concerned with what ought to be rather than with what is or must be. In other words, it is something normative. But the norm in question is anything but natural reason. Law, said Kelsen, is a sanctioned order, that is, a directive which should be obeyed. It matters not whence the order arises, whether it be from an individual leader, a democratic State or society in general. Neither is it of import whence the sanction stems; this can vary from society to society and from period to period. In the Middle Ages it derived mainly from the consent of the people; in modern times it derives mainly from the police; in primitive society it comes from the mores of the community.

Law, as a sanctioned directive, is concerned with what ought to be, not an ought which springs from any kind of morality or natural order, but rather from what Kelsen called its *Grundnorm*, a kind of categorical imperative in the domain of legality. The *Grundnorm* can vary from system to legal system. In one it can take the classical form associated with statist positivism: "Commands of the sovereign are to be obeyed". In another it can carry the overtones of a nationalistic positivism, as in the case of the *Führerprinzip* of Hitler's Germany. In communistic positivism its form will be along the lines that class interests are to be secured, and so on for other forms. Never, but never, can it have anything to do with the principle "Good is to be done and evil avoided". That is morality not legality; it is the fruit of the categorical imperative in the individual order, the conscience of the isolated individual. Legality springs from an analogous but quite distinct categorical imperative and it is this which Kelsen terms its *Grundnorm*. For him "the basic norm of a legal order is the postulated ultimate rule according to which the proximate norms of this order are established and annulled, receive and lose their validity". In short the *Grundnorm* is a necessary hypothesis, on the basis of which the legislator can carry on his work and the citizen extend his obedience. It is precisely because Kelsen's theory covers every variety of positivism, since it leaves room for different basic norms in different societies, and also in fact for a basic norm in international society (such as *Pacta sunt servanda*), that the theory has been called the *"Pure Theory of Law"*. It escapes, as it were, from the concrete characteristics that qualify the different particular legal systems.

Ingenious though it is, Kelsen's theory of law failed to escape the major objection which confronts all positivism. I refer again to the inability of positivism to preserve legality from degenerating into arbitrariness. As a system of formal logic applied to law it is incontestable; of course it is necessary to ground legal structures upon a basic premise, norm or value or whatever else one may call it. The trouble with Kelsen's theory is that the norms (or *Grundnorm*) of different societies are themselves basically factual and therefore positive. As such they could only be adequate if they in turn rested on some further basis—or hypothesis—that is not itself positive. Kelsen himself actually leaves room for such:

> That a norm of the kind just mentioned is the basic norm of the national legal order does not imply that it is impossible to go beyond that norm. Certainly one may ask why one has to respect the first constitution as a binding norm. The answer might be that the fathers of the first constitution were empowered by God. The characteristic of so-called legal positivism is, however, that it dispenses with any such religious justification of the legal order. The basic norm is only the necessary presupposition of any positivistic interpretation of legal material. (*General Theory of Law and the State, 1920*).

This is interesting for it allows legal positivism—as a limited theory of law—to be accepted by people whose general philosophy is strongly committed to defending theism and morality. It permits them to be positivists in legal theory while adhering to a non-positivist position in other domains. There have been many such in the ranks of Catholics. One thinks, for example, of the Louvain jurist Jean Dabin whose *Théorie Générale du Droit* (1944) postulated the existence of ethical principles which could be used by law but refused to incorporate them into legal theory to the extent that they might be called legal principles.

The big trouble with Kelsen's theory—as a legal phil-osophy—is that a pure hypothesis does not suffice as a rational basis for law. There is all the difference in the world between Kelsen and Aquinas, for whom the law of the State rests on the ultimate foundation of the will of God as creator, in which the natural law is a proximate participation. In and through this it finds both its limit and its power of obligation. It is true that for Kelsen, equally with Aquinas, the juridical order is not just a matter of human will. For both a superior norm is necessary before positive law can exist as law. But whereas for Aquinas this norm is objective and absolute, for Kelsen it is hypothetical and relative. At best it might be described as something relatively absolute but even as such it cannot escape being arbitrary. What I am saying is that, despite its fixity as the basis of each particular system of law, the *Grundnorm* idea is such that it can be employed to justify any legal system. As Kelsen himself put it: "It implies no categorical statement as to the value of the method of law-making or of the person functioning as the positive legal authority". This is merely saying in other words that the *Pure Theory of Law* abstains altogether from making a judgement about any particular system, its approach to law or the content of its laws. And it does so on the grounds that to introduce considerations from outside the system or to want to change the system or to refuse to obey within the system, would be to introduce heterogenous elements pertaining to morality or politics that are not pertinent to the theory of law.

The law is the law and ought to be obeyed, irrespective of what its content may be. This would seem to be the essence of Kelsen's theory. And if one were to search for a general note which is always and everywhere characteristic of the *Grundnorm*, it would seem to be a kind of Germanic principle—"Follow the Law". The meaning of it all is that, in spite of its efforts to avoid this, Kelsen's theory provides no limit to the power of the State.

It is not surprising therefore that events should have proven that statist positivism was bound to lead to legal arbitrariness. Nor is it strange that the most extreme example came from Germany. Early on in the Hitler régime, in June, 1935, a law of the Third Reich laid down that in future juridical procedure should not be in accordance with a *fixed law* but rather in accordance with an *instinctive* appreciation of what the good of the people required. The Rule of Law was no more. And it took little time for the results of emerge. Already, in executing Ernest Roehm and his colleagues without any due process or trial, Hitler had laid down the principle that anything is justified when it is "an act of self-defence of the State". "In that hour", he said, "I was responsible for the fate of the German nation and thereby the supreme law-Lord of the German people". Later he was to carry much further his concept of what the self-defence of the State entailed:

> We are obliged to depopulate as part of our mission of preserving the German population. We shall have to develop a technique of depopulation. If you ask me what I mean by depopulation, I mean the removal of entire racial units. And that is what I intend to carry out—that, roughly, is my task. If I can send the flower of the German nation into the hell of war without the smallest pity for the spilling of precious German blood, then surely I have the right to remove millions of an inferior race that breeds like vermin.

Himmler wrote in similar vein, even when by way of qualification:

> Obviously in such a mixture of peoples as the Slavs there will always be some racially good types. Therefore I think it is our duty to take their children with us, to remove them from their environment, if necessary by robbing or stealing them . . . . . Either we win over any good that we can use for ourselves and give it a place in our people or . . . . we destroy this blood.

It is interesting to note that, although they were enemies, the Third Reich and the U.S.S.R. had much in common in the domain of legal theory and practice. For both, a denial of natural law conduced to a legal positivism that entailed the arbitrary treatment of the individual by the State. In accordance with its force theory of the State, Marxist philosophy regards law as the instrument of politics. In an article "The Theory of the State and Law", published in *Soviet Legal Philosophy* in 1951, the jurists Golunski and Stragovich described law as something which safeguards "arrangements agreeable and advantageous to the dominant class"—a concept remarkably similar to that put forward by Trasymachus in antiquity. It was this theory of law which found its first official expression in a Soviet Decree of 12th September, 1919, which defined law as "a set of rules for social relationships, which corresponds to the interests of the dominant class, and is safeguarded by the organized force of that class". There is no need to recall the enormities which were perpetrated under the aegis of this Communist legal positivism.

The fourth and final form of positivism in law is that which I have called sociological positivism. In a general way its origins go back to Comte, but he himself did not believe that juridical matters were capable of development along the lines of empirical sociology. He considered the jurists as being too closely associated with the metaphysicians and moralists, too concerned with norms to permit of their subject being treated positively. His successors, however, have effected this by way of the study of the effective functioning of legal institutions. For the sociological positivists, juridical reality, i.e. law, rests neither on the command of the State nor on that of a higher law but rather on the respect and obedience which in actual fact is given to it by society. In other words, one looks at the receiving end rather than the giving end when seeking for the criterion of law. As the French jurist Jezé has put it: "The law of a country is the ensemble of rules—good or bad, useful or harmful—which, at a given moment, are effectively applied by legal practitioners and tribunals". And the American Justice Holmes conveyed the same ideas by saying that "law is a prophecy concerning what the courts of justice do in reality". What he meant is that law is a verbal formulation of the existing pattern of social behaviour. It is not so much something which dominates and fashions conduct as a resultant of majority ways of acting. In short, the *Lex facit regem* of Bracton has come to have an entirely new meaning and application. Instead of signifying, as it did originally, that the ruler receives the law from above, if employed at all it would now mean that the ruler receives the law exclusively from below. His function as the declarer rather than maker of law, is to engage in forecasting about the path society is likely to follow. And just as some present-day planning consultants do not hesitate to affix the term "plan" to studies which are really the negation of plans, being simply elaborate expositions of the way in which regions have been developing and are likely to develop over the years, in the same way the juridical positivists have no qualms about calling "law" what is truly only a framework which caters for the way in which people in general want to act and not at all something which directs their action into channels which have been determined by the legislator. A good example is the law governing trade unions which, in the interpretation of the sociological positivists, is the fruit of a developing society whereby the juridical integument kept pace with the train of events which could not conceivably have been stopped even if the legislators—as they were in the early days of the Combination Acts—were disposed to keep the clock from moving on.

The method of sociological legal positivism, therefore, is to seek positive factual and institutional bases for legal principles rather than seek to mould the former by way of the latter. It contrasts sharply with the method of morals whereby principles are outlined as a basis for conduct and institutions. There is all the difference in the world between the ethical approach to problems of the family, for example, and the entirely factual approach of empirical sociology. In the same way, there is a world of difference between a normative approach to law and what is called the realistic approach of sociological legal positivism.

The growth of this positivism has been rapid due to the convergence of a number of factors. In the first place, of course, there was the modern tendency towards positivism in every sphere. Secondly, you had the influence of Savigny's Historical School of Law, which from the early decades of the last century, had been underlining the importance of historical facts in the shaping of law. Thirdly, there was the impact of Gierke, whose emphasis on the role of the community in the fashioning of law tended sometimes to be a little *de trop*. But the main thrust behind the emergence of sociological positivism in law was undoubtedly an endeavour to find a way of curbing the power of the State which the other kinds of positivism had failed to do. And the bedrock idea was that law should be conceived as something which obliges and should oblige by reason of its content rather than its origin. It obliges only if it is in the interests of, and is accepted by the community—not just because it happens to be imposed. And just as a bad political system breaks down through revolt when people decide to have done with it, so also a poor legal measure breaks down by the refusal of the people to obey it. Or by their refusal to extend it obedience in the first instance. The supreme example of this, which the sociological positivists love to recall, is the failure of the prohibition laws in America.

Perhaps the best-known exponent of sociological legal positivism was the French jurist Leon Duguit. In his major work *Traité de Droit Constitutionnel* (1921–26) he vigorously opposed statist positivism which, he said, rested on the erroneous presupposition of the deified State, becoming in Germany, in the years between 1870 and 1914, "a legal screen for organized oppression" and which was incapable of being controlled by "verbiage" about the auto-limitation of the State. How, he asked rightly, can the State be limited by law if it can modify law at its own good pleasure? Law should rather be defined as that which sets limits to the State. The following quotation illustrates Duguit's position:

> The Governors are individuals like others, subject like other individuals to the rules of law founded on a social and intersocial solidarity. These rules of law impose on them their duties, and their acts will be legitimate and will impose obedience . . . . when and only when they are in conformity with the rules of law which bind them.
>
> Neither an emperor, nor a king, nor a parliament, nor a popular majority, can impose their will as such: their acts can bind the governed only if they are in conformity with law.
>
> The positive legislator has no power to create law; he can only state what it is and issue constructive prescriptions to put it into force. The logical consequence of this is that a law which is contrary to objective law . . . . is an invalid law, a law without executive force.

One could so easily be deceived by all this into believing that one was back again in the days of Cicero, of Augustine, Aquinas or Bracton. The phrases are certainly similar in many places but the import is entirely different. The "objective law" in question is not at all the natural law; Duguit as a materialist and positivist would have none of this. The objective law of which he spoke was rather the fruit of an argument to the effect that since man can only live in society, there must exist a series of rules for the maintenance of order within it. Rules, that is, which impose themselves and these he identified with the social norms which are continually emerging within society. Law is therefore essentially something social; it springs from and redounds to society. This indeed is the difference between Duguit and the natural law theorists. For him human solidarity constitutes the ultimate basis of law; its exigencies are revealed by custom which reflects its interests. Law is simply the formulation of these. The same is true, for the positivists, in the case of economic and moral regulations; the only difference is that juridical regulations carry sanctions.

Legal sanction is the organized coercive reaction of the group to violations of custom and law. It is on this point that sociological legal positivism breaks down as an effort to limit the power of the State. For seeing that it is the State itself that formulates the custom into law, represents and commands the coercive force to implement it, and indeed creates the form of the sanction itself by way of law, law cannot effectively limit the State. Like all positivism, sociological positivism fails in this by reason of conceiving law exclusively in terms of society. For Duguit, as for sociological legal positivists generally, the centre of gravity of law is placed in the dispositions of mind, opinions and aspirations of the people who make up the collectivity of society. There is no *a priori* conception of a "given" law; anything can change at any given time.

There is a remarkable likeness between these ideas and particular notions about law in the Church which one sometimes finds floating around today. There is a genre of literature, calling itself the theology of law, which—against the perspective of a post-Conciliar ecclesiology—seeks to root Church law so intimately and uniquely in the community as to forget the role of authority in law-making. Law becomes not so much the instrument of the Hierarchy for the promotion of the common good as the instrument of the community for its self-development. As such it is seen as backed less by Christ's command when instituting ecclesial authority, *Whatsoever you shall bind . . .* than by Christ seen as sacrament of the charismatically infallible community, *Wherever two or three of you are gathered in my name . . .*

Such an approach is but a variation of the self-same theme as has been cropping up constantly in the course of these pages. What I mean is that we are in the presence of a concept of law which is a kind of "collectivization" of the product of the individual conscience as defended by situation ethics. The institutional element of authority has been destructuralized. But only to the accompaniment of serious difficulties. If law can change with the mood of the community, the community is not really under law at all. Once again, and in a new and unusual domain, the road to arbitrariness is open. Secondly, as we shall see presently, any community cannot subsist for long without the support of a legal institution which is imposed on it. In the Church, the People of God conscious of itself and of its needs as a community, can no more do without law and the authority of the Hierarchy than can secular society avoid anarchy without an institutional framework that is not dependent on community whim. There is a point beyond which the theory of democracy holds no water—something that is true in both Church and secular society.

119

9

8

Positivism in Morals:
Conscientious Licence?

FOR SOME years now a growing tendency within the Church has been to elevate conscience into the only really significant criterion of morality. To be sure, owing to the place which objective standards, natural law and authoritative teaching have always held in traditional Catholic thought, an effort is usually made to promote conscience in a way that is duly subordinate to these.

A good example of this is to be found in the writings of Father Charles E. Curran, Professor of Moral Theology at the Catholic University of America. But it is becoming increasingly difficult to maintain this effort while successfully avoiding "doublethink". In his first book, *Christian Morality Today*, published from Notre Dame in 1966, Father Curran wrote as follows:

> Every concrete situation is unique. The Christian's answer to the divine call must correspond to his individual circumstances. Conscience is a supernatur-

120

ally elevated subjective power of man. The law of Christ and the natural law are primarily internal laws. Why then is it necessary to have detailed, particular, external expressions of these laws? . . . . Particular, external expressions of the law of love and natural law have a value only insofar as they point out the minimum and basic demands of the law of love (pp. 19–20) . . . . .

After prayerful consideration of all the factors involved, the Christian chooses what he believes to be the demands of love in the present situation . . . . . For the Christian who has made a commensurate effort to form his conscience correctly, the dictate of conscience is an infallible norm of conduct. Even though the action itself is not in conformity with the divine will, the Christian's conduct is pleasing to God, for it stems from a pure heart (pp. 21–22).

In a second book, *A New Look at Christian Morality,* which appeared two years later (Notre Dame, 1968), while continuing to affirm the existence of the natural law, Father Curran favoured a radical revision of the whole concept:

The Catholic Church and Catholic theology is not irreparably committed to accept the natural law as a coherent system for the understanding of moral conduct (p. 86) . . . . .

The changing concept of the theology of the Church and authority in the Church also calls for a change in the role of law in the Church. Law in the Church has only an ancillary function. The source of all life in the Church remains the Holy Spirit who dwells in the hearts of all . . . . . Individual responsibility, creativity, and initiative are much more important than mere conformity to an elaborate system of law. The realisation of the secondary role of law in the life of the Church will necessarily have repercussions on the emphasis on law in moral theology (p. 101).

It is relevant here to note that there can be little doubt that Father Curran was by now under considerable influence from considerations arising out of the birth control controversy. He had in fact hoisted the flag in support of its liceity in conditions to be judged by the conscience of the married. It was only to be expected, therefore, that the issuing of the encyclical *Humanae Vitae*, with its rejection of this position, should have evoked a critical reaction from Father Curran and a still more critical attitude towards natural law on which the papal decision had been grounded. These he provided in a third book, entitled *Absolutes in Moral Theology*, published hard on the heels of the encyclical in 1968. In it we read:

> The recent papal encyclical presupposes a natural law concept that fails to indicate the relative and provisional character of natural law in the total Christian perspective. (p. 157) . . . . .

> In the context of the contemporary scene in moral theology, Catholic thinkers have been analyzing and criticizing the concept of natural law, especially understood as it is in *Humanae Vitae* . . . . . The natural law does not refer to a coherent philosophical theory with an agreed body of ethical content in existence from the beginning of time . . . . . Natural law in the history of thought does not refer to a monolithic theory, but tends to be a more generic term which includes a number of different approaches to moral problems (p. 168).

[Some people, he says, would in fact prefer to abandon the term altogether because of its ambiguity and adopt a more personalist approach of a kind which would allow contraception in certain circumstances.]

There is no denying that views like those of Father Curran are not to be classed as situationist in the ordinary sense. Indeed they are designed to avoid situationism. How different they are from this will be realized quickly if one collates them with the views of a Joseph Fletcher or a John A. Robinson. These latter, while admitting the fact of a moral law, are at pains to say that it is unimportant when compared to love. Writes Fletcher: "What a difference it makes when love is the only norm (in contrast to a morality of laws and rules). How free and responsible we are". (*Situation Ethics*, Philadelphia, 1966, p. 80). And Robinson in his *Christian Morals Today* (Philadelphia, 1964) admits the relevance of law in theory only.

Situationism had its origins in the world of evangelical theologians like Barth, coupled with the post-war ideas of existentialist philosophers. Barth firmly rejected all types of ethics based on a fixed set of rules or commands of God which the individual simply applied in concrete circumstances. For him human conscience and human conscience alone, is the only organ through which the living word of the Lord Jesus Christ speaks to man in the power of the Holy Spirit. All his references to the all-abiding "commands of God" must be understood in the frame of reference of conscience. Needless to say, it is not difficult to see how such sentiments could be carried to an extreme of moral relativism. Particularly when linked with existentialist concepts.

This in fact is what was done—and quickly—both by Protestant and some Catholic writers. As with Father Curran, there was an attempt at the beginning to have it both ways, when for example Reinhold Niebuhr wrote:

> In so far as man has a determinate structure, it is possible to state the "essential nature" of his existence to which his actions ought to conform and which they should fulfill. But in so far as he has the freedom to transcend structure, standing beyond himself and beyond every particular social situation, every law is subject to indeterminate possibilities which finally exceed the limits of any specific definition of what he ought to do (*Theology Studies*, 28, p. 226).

In the same way Fletcher has written:

> Situation ethics goes part of the way with natural law, by accepting reason as the instrument of moral judgement, while rejecting the notion that good is "given" in the nature of things, objectively. It goes part of the way with Scriptural law by accepting revelation as the source of the norm while rejecting all "revealed" norms or laws but the one command —to love God in the neighbour. The situationist follows a moral law or violates it according to love's need (*Situation Ethics*, p. 26).

But it is well-nigh impossible to maintain such nuances for long and at times the wood appears through the trees. As when Fletcher, in *The Commonweal*, for 14 June, 1966, wrote "Love is the only measure".

It was its proneness to relativism that had caused situation ethics to be censured in a number of utterances by Pope Pius XII. Two such were the Addresses of 23 March and 24 April, 1952. Despite this, quite a number of Catholic moralists are in agreement with views like

Fletcher's. Father Louis Mondern, a Belgian Jesuit, writing in *Sin, Liberty and Law,* has declared openly that "we must clearly affirm with the great classical authors that Catholic morality is in fact situation ethics". And Father Thomas Wassmer, S.J., of America has come to the same material conclusion by finding that intrinsic evil is not "a viable term" (Cf. Harvey Cox, *The Situation Ethics Debate,* Philadelphia, 1968).

But these are rather extreme expressions of the movement within the Catholic Church towards some form of *rapprochement* with situationism. One of the best known representatives of a more moderate approach has been the German Jesuit, Father Joseph Fuchs. In articles in the *Nouvelle Revue Théologique* during the years 1954 and 1956 Father Fuchs maintained that the application of general norms to concrete situations must necessarily mean "a morality of the *kairos*" or moment of absolute originality (See also K. Rahner, "Situationethik und Sundenmystik" in *Stimmen der Zeit,* 1949–50 and "Über die Frage einer formalen Existentialethik" in *Schriften zur Theologie,* II, Einsiedeln, 1955). The same ideas have been continued in more recent years by others, for example, Karl Rahner's idea of an "existential ethics". By this he means an ethic of prudence whereby the individual "makes his own decisions freely within his nature, i.e. the whole complex of all the conditioning elements, grace included, which make up his humanity" (Cited in Franz Furger, "Prudence and Moral Change", in *Concilium,* vol. 35, New York, 1968, p. 127). For "there is a moral individuality of a positive kind which cannot be fitted into a simple general ethics; there is something unique which is nevertheless morally binding" (*Ibid.* p. 127). As one commentator has put it, these decisions stem from a wholly personal imperative that includes both natural elements and the call of God's grace which man expresses in his concrete situation. "Accord-

125

ing to Rahner, this specific insight is due to prudence, which is here understood as both naturally acquired and as a gift of the Spirit. Therefore it becomes, so to speak, a kind of flair for what God wants me to do precisely here and now" (Furger, *loc. cit.*, p. 128).

The following is one further expression of the same thing:

> Prudence occupied a prominent position in Aristotle's system of ethics, and was taken over by St Thomas into his theological synthesis. Aristotelian prudence is in fact the virtue of judging action on the basis of experience . . . . . With the acceleration of history, retrospective prudence is no longer sufficient. Not only is it possible for the present situation to have no precedents that can have been registered by experience, but it is certain that the future will contain a number of elements that cannot be foreseen now. Therefore, for prudence to be really prudent today, it must become a firmly prospective virtue. And Aristotelian prudence must of course be complemented by a theology of Christian time, of the *kairos* as an *absolutely original* moment in which God is revealing himself to man and arousing an adequate and generous response in him through his grace (J. Lobo, "Toward a Morality Based on the Meaning of History", in *Understanding the Signs of the Times, Concilium*, vol. 25, 1967).

A variant of the same position has been developed by Father Bernard Haering around the central idea of love. For Haering moral value is nothing if not person offering and accepting love. Norms and laws are based upon this value; as Haering puts it: "Value dictates norm" (Cf. *The Law of Christ*, vol. I, p. 227). Love and love alone recognizes the proper order of values, a love that is not merely human but the love of the Holy Spirit.

For Haering, therefore, the centre of value is what he calls the "Value-Person" (*die Wertperson*). It is interesting to note the close resemblance between this basic criterion of morality and the *Grundnorm* of legality proposed by Kelsen. At least as basic criteria they are very much the same. So much so that the criticism which we have levelled at the latter, on the grounds of ignoring natural law in favour of a positive pattern of political legality, seems equally applicable to the former on the grounds of its basing morality on the decisions of the individual, even if they are conscientious decisions inspired by love. For love of its nature is arbitrary in a way that law is not.

It is quite true, of course, that, like the others, Father Haering does not profess to reject law. And least of all a law of nature. Father Charles Curran has summed up his position as follows:

> In general, Haering accepts the traditional Catholic understanding of the natural law, but he incorporates the natural law into his more biblically inspired, dialogical understanding of the Christian life . . . . . Within the large field of human actions which are compatible with our human nature, there are no general principles from which man can always deduce what is the fitting thing to do. Under the inspiration of the Spirit man is led to embrace those actions which are most fitting in the particular situation. (*A New Look at Christian Morality*, p. 154).

As with the others, however, one is compelled to feel that at the level of practice, such an outlook on natural law very quickly reduces itself to a lip service that could be compatible with arbitrariness. "Love and do what thou wilt" is a high principle that does not always safeguard against licence. Possibly with a view to avoiding this, a number of contemporary expositions of the morality of conscience seek to assign a heightened place to the community in influencing the decisions of the individual. Some do this by recommending that the moral teaching of the Church should always be fashioned in a living context of community. One writer has called for "a dialogical magisterium" (Daniel C. Maguire, "Moral Absolutes and the Magisterium", in C. Curran ed. *Absolutes in Moral Theology*, pp. 102–107). And Fr. Curran has written that "the teaching authority of the Church must be willing to test the experience of individuals against the background of the whole community" (*A New Look at Christian Morality*, p. 97).

But all agree that morality cannot stem from democratic choice only and that it is vitally necessary to exercise care to preclude this. One of the writers just quoted, Father Daniel Maguire, stresses that the Church must not "succumb to the weakness of consensus politics" (*loc. cit.*, p. 104). The other, Father Curran, says: "I do believe that there is a basic truth in natural law theory that must be preserved. Morality can never become a matter of whim or caprice, but must always correspond to reality" (*Christian Morality Today*, p. 89).

Father Curran is optimistic that it should be eminently possible to find a way of ensuring this while preserving the role of the community. He claims, in fact, that throughout history "the experience of Christian people seems to have been the primary factor in the change of traditional teaching" (*Op. cit.*, p. 89). He adds: "If Christian experience is so important, what is going to happen to the teaching authority of the Church? If individual experience is the ultimate criterion, is the door not opened for pure subjectivism and anarchy? I do not think so . . . . . (Since) the magisterial or teaching Church reflects the experience of the Christian people, on some occasions the teaching Church will be behind the times" (p. 90).

One is forced to wonder, however, whether such confidence is entirely justified. One further quotation will suffice to give an example of how liberty without law can border on licence:

> The principle of love must be worked out in detail by each Christian in a manner suitable to his own situation and his own resources, for ultimately no one except the person who loves knows whether his love is genuine and full. It is not for another to impose a ceiling on his love. Nor is it for another to teach how to love, since love is an action that cannot be taught as history and geometry are taught. It is communicated by love received, by love shown in example, by "immersion in an atmosphere of love," which ought to be the atmosphere of the Christian community.
>
> That the annulment of obligation is a consequence of the annulment of the law I deduce from the fact that no other law is substituted for the law of Judaism. The Christian will do the acts of love from the motivation of love or they are not Christian acts . . . . . If one thinks of morality as comprised of love instead of law, it is extremely difficult to define a point at which one has done all that one ought. Love is not considered in terms of what one ought to do.

In evading freedom, Catholics evade responsibility. They permit the character of their Christian fulfilment to be determined by another. Where they ought to look for leadership they look for control, and it must be said that they have little trouble in finding it. By doing so they renounce the freedom to act as

129

a religious subject. This can be ultimately the renunciation of Christian love. I am optimistic enough
to think that discontent with this type of managed
Christianity will grow, and that more and more
people will see that they will be as free as they
insist on being (John L. McKenzie, S.J., "The
Freedom of the Christian", in C. B. Ketchem and
J. F. Day ed., *Faith and Freedom: Essays in Contemporary Theology*, New York, 1969).

Here we are not far from a Kantian-type of morality,
entirely autonomous in character. For unless something
"given" by "another" is admitted in the matter, one has
a denial of heterogeneity *à la* Kant. We have seen how
this conduced to arbitrariness in the field of legality. Is
there any less reason for thinking that the same would be
the result in that of morality? The protection of community sanction is no protection. "Laws in order to command
respect", writes the English Catholic jurist, Peter Benen-
son, "must coincide with the general will of the people
. . . . . The true concept of natural law is that in inherent
compliance with his predestined function to create order
out of chaos, man seeks to create ever-widening communities. From this it follows that anything which is
conducive to the stability and ultimate growth of a community . . . . is in accordance with natural law" (Cf. "The
Natural Law and Statute Law" in *Understanding the
Signs of the Times, Concilium,* vol. 24, pp. 34, 47 and 57).
Words, words, words, as Rousseau's doctrine of the
general will has so clearly proved in practice. The stark
implications of such autonomous community attitudes
have been brought to our notice in the report *A Quaker
View of Sex* (London, 1963):

We cannot accept as true a statement that is given
us merely because it is given with the authority of

tradition or of a Church. We have to make that truth our own, if it is a truth, through diligent search and rigorous discipline of thought and feeling. Man is intended to be a moral being. That is not to say that he should accept a formal morality, an observance of mores, but that his actions should come under serious scrutiny in the light that comes to us from the Gospels and the working of God in us . . . . . This search is a move forward into the unknown; it implies a high standard of responsibility, thinking and awareness—something harder than simple obedience to a moral code. Further, the responsibility that it implies cannot be accepted alone, it must be responsibility within a group whose members are equally committed to the search for God's will (p. 41).

The proof of the pudding as regards what extremes can result from this kind of thinking, is contained in the subsequent envisaging by the same report that certain forms of behaviour could be moral which have always hitherto been accepted as licentious.

9

Towards the Rehabilitation of Natural Law

THE FATAL consequences of the abandonment of natural law have made themselves felt most keenly in the realm of legality. This, after all, is not surprising, as it is in this realm that the influence of positivism was earliest experienced and the fruits of its inevitable arbitrariness first reaped. Sufficient time has not elapsed for a similar realization of the consequences of natural law rejection for morality. But it is the argument of the present book that, if a lesson can be learned from what has happened as regards legality, a determined effort should be made to rehabilitate natural law concepts and thereby avoid the arbitrary decisions of the individual conscience which are otherwise likely to masquerade as morality.

For this reason the contemporary juridical quest for natural law is of enormous interest to and importance for the moralist. The beginnings of this quest can be traced to the years of the Second World War when the perpetration of enormities in the name of law first became painfully prominent. The Nuremberg Trials, immediately after the war, brought it to a head. The main interest of Nuremberg centres around the fact that the German defence was on a basis of legal philosophy. There was no denial that the defendants had placed the acts with which they were charged, terrible though these acts might have been. What was denied, and denied strongly in the name of legal theory, was that these acts constituted crimes and were punishable. "We broke no law", said the accused, "and therefore we are not legally guilty". And the extraordinary thing is that, according to the legal philosophy which both they and their accusers accepted, this was in fact the case. It needed a revival of natural law concepts and the introduction of a charge of breaking that law to make it possible to convict and sentence them. But let us look at the matter in a little greater detail.

In all, the German defendants at Nuremberg were charged with being guilty of three kinds of crime. These crimes were crimes against peace, war crimes and crimes against humanity. The Nuremberg tribunal itself defined what they meant. Crimes against peace were described as the "planning, preparation, initiation or waging of a war of aggression, or a war in violation of international treaties". Similarly, war crimes were described as "violations of the laws or customs of war". Finally, crimes against humanity were described as "murder, extermination, enslavement, deportation and other inhuman acts committed against any civilian population". One should note carefully an important difference between these descriptions. Whereas in the case of crimes against peace and war crimes respectively, "international treaties" and "laws of war" are given as criteria, in the case of crimes against humanity no such touchstone is mentioned. Natural law was the only candidate for this and when Nuremberg opened it was recognized by none of the parties as law.

On the legal positivist premises on which the Nuremberg tribunal rested, the accused could possibly be convicted of having broken only two laws—national and international. For in positivist theory all law derives either from the *fiat* of a given State or from an agreement between States to which each has extended its assent. No other *radix* of law is known to positivism. It was the German claim, in accordance with this, that the defendants were innocent since it was hard to see how they had broken any law. They had carried out that of the Third Reich rather than ignored it and, as far as international treaties went, while it is true that Germany had been party to the Fourth Hague Convention of 1907 and the General Treaty for the Renunciation of War of 27th August, 1928 —both of which excluded the waging of armed conflict— on 14th October, 1933, she had left the League of Nations and the International Disarmament Conference. In other words, she had withdrawn her assent to the consensus on which the international laws underwriting crimes against peace and war crimes positively rested.

Because of this, only very tenuously could the Nuremberg defendants be charged with crimes that demanded a positive basis on international law. And, on reading the accounts of the trial, one cannot help getting the feeling that this was realized fully by at least some of the prosecutors. One begins to see how necessary it was for them to introduce some other basis of charge into the business. It was in this context that crimes against humanity made their appearance, very mixed up, albeit, with talk of crimes against peace and war crimes, since these alone had any semblance of juridical basis. A member of the British prosecution, Sir David Maxwell-Fyfe, has left us a classical example of this confusion, however unintended: "With regard to 'crimes against humanity' this at any rate is clear: the Nazis when they persecuted and murdered countless Jews and political opponents in Germany,

knew that what they were doing was wrong and that
their actions were crimes which had been condemned by
the criminal law of every civilized State. When these
crimes were mixed with the preparation of aggressive war
and later with the commission of war crimes in occupied
territories, it cannot be a matter of complaint that a
procedure is established for their punishment".

In short, it was the submission of the prosecution at
Nuremberg that, even if it were not crystal clear that the
accused were indeed guilty of having broken national or
international laws by which they were bound at the time
of their actions, they were still open to conviction on the
ground of being guilty of what was loosely termed
"crimes against humanity". How loosely can be judged
from the preceding quotation. For when there is no law
there cannot be a crime and on British, French, Russian
and American principles, as much as German, there was
no such thing as a natural law the breaking of which
would constitute crime as such. Hence the plea of the defendants to the effect that they had broken no law and
could therefore not be charged with any crime. On the
score of legality, as understood by positivists, they were
in the clear. As Dr. Jahrreis, counsel for General Jodl,
put it: "In a State in which the entire power to make
final decisions is concentrated in the hands of a single
individual, the orders of this one man are absolutely
binding on the members of the hierarchy . . . . . This
individual is their sovereign . . . . they have neither the
right nor the duty to examine the orders of the monocrat
to determine their legality". And if Matthias Drefregger,
Auxiliary Bishop of Munich, upright and conscientious
man that he surely must have been, could say that at
that same moment of history he could have given certain
orders, later regarded by others as criminal, while feeling
himself "legally but above all morally not guilty", are we
not compelled to admit that at the time it must have been

extremely difficult for people to have grasped fully the legal implications of their actions.

Yet the accused at Nuremberg, as we know, were condemned as being guilty—primarily—of crimes against humanity. The ironical thing is that in deciding this, the court necessarily implied that they had violated one law or another. And it had to be a law other than national or international. Justice Robert Jackson, using the words of Coke and Bracton when summing up, said that the tribunal showed "a faith that even rulers are under God and the Law". It had applied, he said "what has sometimes been called a natural law".

There you have the nub of the matter—the Nuremberg tribunal being compelled to return to natural law in order to escape the unacceptable consequences of legal positivism. As I have said before, there had been a growing tendency in this direction from the early years of World War II. In 1942 the great American jurist Roscoe Pound had said that "something like a resurrection of natural law is going on the world over . . . . . Philosophical Jurisprudence which was all but extinct fifty years ago has revived and taken the lead in the present century". This development has continued since the war. In 1949 the *American Bar Association Journal* put it as follows: "Today the critical problems and confusions which our great transition is forcing upon us compel us again to turn to natural law for eternal values and ideas of universal application".

It is currently possible to say without fear of contradiction that something similar is greatly to be desired in the sphere of morality.

By now, however, it should be clear to everybody that any rehabilitation of natural law—whether in the sphere of legality or that of morality—must take account of the changing pattern of life to a far greater extent than was customary in the past. Particular care must be exercised to escape the straitjacket of an entirely inflexible universal natural law. We have delved sufficiently into the history of this concept to realize that, more than any thing else, it has been responsible for the decay of the natural law.

It is for this reason that an emphasis on experience is of paramount importance in any effort to restore natural law thinking. For this will ensure that one leaves adequate room for variation in natural law—variation at least to some extent, within a respect for unchanging basic principles. And quite frankly, in saying this, one is saying nothing more than Aquinas intended when he conceived the natural law as capable of variation in its secondary principles. For these are but applications of the primary principles to the variegated existential facts of life. The secondary principles in turn can themselves be applied to a further range of data whereby still more conclusions— or tertiary principles—can be deduced.

It should be noted carefully that, as Aquinas saw things, this process of application—whether leading to secondary, tertiary or even more remote principles of natural law— is neither a pure *a priori* rationalistic exercise drawing out the implications of an essence, nor yet a pure *a posteriori* empirical surveying. It is a combination of rationalism and empiricism by way of which the implications of the basic inclinations of man in his ever-changing historical situation are drawn out.

This, as we have seen, means that the natural law is open to development, to progress. Whether by way of addition (such as the contemporary moral imperative to foster international society) or by way of subtraction (such as the dropping of the institution of slavery), it is and has got to be adaptable.

During the course of Vatican II a controversy about this erupted in Rome between the Canadian theologian Father Gregory Baum and Dr. C. B. Daly, of Queen's University, Belfast, now Bishop of Ardagh and Clonmacnoise. The controversy was occasioned by a pamphlet on birth control, which had been published by Dr. Daly, *Natural Law Morality Today* (Dublin, 1965). Father Baum launched a critique based on natural law ideas. Although what he had to say did not do justice to what it was intended to criticize—since this had, in fact, envisaged a progressive moral development—it was the occasion of an exposition of the question of natural law which in precise terms expressed the heart of the problem. We cannot do better than quote Father Baum:

> There are, in fact, two views of natural law, both of which are traditional, both of which are found in the writings of St. Thomas, even if they cannot easily be harmonised.
>
> According to one view, natural law is the set of moral principles derived from a rational grasp of human nature. Man can be defined. We know his essence. From this essence philosophical reason is able to derive external and unchanging principles of human behaviour.
>
> According to the other view, the so-called natural laws are the moral principles discovered by man in history, involved in following his destiny, who is willing to reflect rationally on his own experience and the experience of mankind. There is something like a common conscience of mankind. To this history gives witness. This common conscience is influenced by cultural and political factors. It is also influenced —at least, this is the Christian conviction—by the destiny to which God has appointed man, the destiny to seek truth and communion.
>
> The first view we may call the logico-rational understanding and the second view the historico-rational understanding of natural law.
>
> In the line of the logico-rational understanding of natural law, Aristotle and St. Thomas were able to

defend the institution of slavery. It was only through the experience of man in history and his rational reflection on this, that the common conscience of mankind rejected the morality of human slavery.

Man reflecting rationally on his experience is constantly discovering new values. As a Christian I believe that the call and the grace of God have something to do with this. A value that has come into the focus of human consciousness in this century, is the dignity of the human person. The Second Vatican Council gives ample evidence of this. The most spectacular example is the declaration on religious liberty. The dignity of the human person is the foundation of his freedom in religious matters. This historical development and our reflection on it, has a great influence on so-called natural law morality; this, at least is true according to the historico-rational understanding of natural law.

Father Baum went on to view the problem of artificial birth control in the light of this understanding:

In the past, the morality of sexuality in married life was derived from biological considerations. The biological integrity of the marriage act was regarded as the moral criterion. The nature of sexuality was regarded the same in man and animals.

Today with a greater appreciation of the human person, many moralists have contested this. They have contested this from moral considerations, precisely because they are convinced of the existence of natural law. They too desire to have objective criteria of human morality. In marriage, they say, which is a communion of life and love, the sexual act must always express and signify the mutual surrender of the two partners in a love that is selfless, healing, creative and fruitful. It would be sinful, against the natural law, to have sexual relations in marriage where the sexual act is robbed of this meaning.

The integrity of the marriage act may be robbed through biological or physiological factors. It may be robbed through a lack of love, through selfishness, through brutality. It need not be robbed in all circumstances through the use of contraceptives. The authors who defend the morality of contraception do uphold natural law, but they have an historico-rational understanding of it. They believe that the moral conscience of mankind has changed in the past, and that on this issue, due to a deeper appreciation of the dignity of the human person, a real change has occurred now (*The Irish Times*, 18 November, 1965).

Needless to say, it is also possible to accept a historico-rational understanding of natural law without necessarily having to accept Father Baum's argument for contraception. The subsequent teaching of *Humanae Vitae* has rejected the conclusions to which his considerations touching human personality led him. It is interesting to note that other writers have mounted a like argument in favour of contraception based on an entirely different range of human experience. One of these is the English Jesuit Father Lionel Keane. In an article on *"The Ambiguity in Natural Law"*, also published in 1965, he wrote:

Catholic moralists, following St. Thomas, do not evaluate the purpose of human sexual intercourse from an actual study of human beings. They deduce it from general principles. Like St. Thomas they classify human sexual intercourse under 'animal' and evaluate it in terms of its animal (biological) function. It is only later they relate it to man's other,

rational, inclinations . . . . . Human sexual intercourse
is more than mere animal copulation, which brings
about procreation. It also brings about emotional,
mental and spiritual union. This is marriage, namely
rational sexual union. The rational element is the
dominant one in man, and it must therefore dominate
the evaluation of all man's actions, including that
of sex.

Once it is accepted that the Church's unrevealed
moral teaching must be based on man's nature and
not on the fixed notions of a bygone age, then the
verified facts of human sexuality . . . . will enable
the Church to adjust her moral code to the present
requirements of man's being. Until recently the con-
tinuance of the human race required a constantly
rising birth-rate. The needs of the human race then
made the biological function of sexual intercourse a
serious obligation. It was then the duty of competent moral authority, e.g. the Catholic Church to
make laws to that effect. When, however, as at
present, over-population threatens the race, the law
of man's being obliges him to curtail the biological
function of sexual intercourse. Competent moral
authority is bound by the natural law to alter its
own laws to secure this end. Although this immediate
relating of moral laws to man's being causes them
to alter as his nature demands, the basis of such
laws—i.e., the structure given to human nature by
God—does not alter. It remains infallibly the same
as He created it (*The Tablet*, 20 March, 1965).

We are not here concerned with the much-debated
question of the morality of artificial contraception. In
the exchange with Father Baum, Dr. Daly declared:

The humanist, personalist and 'developmental'

understanding of natural law has neither an historical nor a logical connection with the moral approval of contraception. It was, as a matter of demonstrable historical fact, elaborated by people who concluded from it to the immorality of contraception. It will not do to go on invoking it as if it were itself a proof of the contrary view (*The Irish Times*, 25 November 1965).

Whatever about the contraception issue, it is certain that natural law theory must allow some room for development in morality. Hence the need for moralists to know the facts about human behaviour in any area about which they are dealing and to integrate this knowledge with their rational insights in elaborating concrete ethical principles. It is true, as Aristotle pointed out of old, that there will always be a degree of uncertainty about their directives. Indeed anything else would be less than human in the sphere in question. Nor should it surprise us if, owing to a progressively better appreciation of the facts relating to any particular problem, moralists differ or change their minds about something.

Modern moralists are in possession of a wide range of fact that was completely unknown to their predecessors. Or rather should we say that the content of sciences like sociology and anthropology is wide open for their inspection and use. Time was when this was not so, in the sense that it was hard to be sure of the value of much nineteenth-century anthropological data. Men like Tylor, Max Muller, Sir James Frazer and others were only too ready to twist the data which the researchers turned up into an argument against traditional positions, especially Christian. It was hard, therefore, to use their findings with confidence. Today all this is changed. Contemporary students of man—with the exception of the Freudians and the Marxists—have no axe to grind that would make

them suspect. Whether atheist or unChristian in their
private beliefs, their empirical studies are generally objective and scholarly. They provide moralists with a full
account of the practices of mankind that could prove of
enormous value in establishing the content of natural law.

It has always been maintained by moralists that the
quasi-universal practice of mankind is a secondary and
manifestative criterion of natural law. Indeed it is precisely because of this that thinkers like the Stoics and
Aquinas regarded the *Jus Gentium* as intimately linked
with natural law. Universally agreed human institutions
and modes of behaviour cannot be ignored when one is
trying to construct a science of ethics.

This, of course, is not to defend a positivistic idea of
morality or a moral relativity that has no room for absolute values. For the positivist, ethics is a purely descriptive science, outlining the mores that are found now
here, now there, in the areas of conduct that are traditionally regarded as those of morality. Customs concerning
marriage or property are prime examples. In the positivist
picture there is no such thing as natural law; morals is
something continually changing and differing from place
to place as it evolves with the condition of men.

The position adopted here is quite otherwise. For one
thing, even if biological evolution were indeed a fact, the
relativity of morals would not necessarily follow. Variation in morality there is and must be; our thesis here is
that it is demanded by natural law, by the concrete application of the absolute values which pertain to man as
such. It is true, no doubt, that a good deal of variation in
moral practice between peoples may be explained in virtue
of their unequal development in reason and civilization—
and this has been an accepted way of explaining it.

Another mode of explanation of the moral variations
between people has been that diversity of circumstances
makes for different ways of applying the same basic and

unchanging moral principles. An example of this is the custom of tribes who kill off their aged, not because they do not respect them or have no regard for life, but on the contrary in order to avoid the cruelty to them that would inescapably be involved by further participation in the hard conditions of tribal life. Certain Bedouin tribes of North Africa, who are continually trekking, have applied the principle of reverence towards parents in this way. Force of circumstances, therefore, has led them to a different conclusion as to what natural law demands in the situation.

Nowadays it is coming to be realized, however, that there is much more to the matter and that moral variations are also—and often—due to the influence of extrinsic factors (economic, social, religious) which prevent people from following what in other circumstances would be a higher form of ethical behaviour. It has come to be realized, for example, that polygamy is predominantly found among peoples whose social conditions (e.g. an imbalance of the sexes), economic requirements (e.g. need for female labour) or religious cults (e.g. ancestor worship) are such as to make a plurality of wives and/or offspring eminently desirable and even necessary. It is not that polygamy is intrinsically as desirable an institution as monogamy, but rather that the force of extrinsic factors is such as to make it acceptable and sometimes even the better thing. From this point of view, it would be correct to say that the practice of polygamy is by no means immoral in all circumstances.

Students of ethics will be quick to notice at least a superficial analogy between the factors which we have here listed as determining morality in practice (less developed reason, circumstances which call for variations in the application of principle and the force of extrinsic factors of all kinds) and the factors (ignorance, concupiscence, fear and violence) which are usually associated with conditioning voluntariety. The difference is that whereas the latter determine the content of subjective morality, the former affect morality objectively. What I mean is that it can be moral and natural for primitive man in the circumstances in which he finds himself to adopt a mode of behaviour which would not be so for the more civilized. It should not be necessary to say that the same is true as between the good pagan and the Christian man. Even between Christians themselves, at different times and in different places, the principle enunciated holds good. Admittedly, it is not easy to know when the circumstances are present to justify a particular practice. It is in this connection that the role of a teaching authority is important. But there should be no mistake about it: natural law is capable of considerable flexibility and anybody who seeks to rehabilitate it in the world of our time must take practical cognisance of this. Law, whether there be question of the juridical or moral order, is compatible with a great deal of diversity. But unless law is respected, even granted this diversity, the only alternative is arbitrariness and licence.

10

The Present Crisis in Society and Church

TO THE sociologist the current emphasis on freedom of conscience in the Church is part of a larger problem which affects society in general. Whether it be the State, economic society, the university or the Church, contemporary man is engaged in a frantic search for greater liberty and the dismantling of structures which hold him down. I think it is fair to say that at the present moment of human history there is a general reaction against social institutions—of which authority is one of the principal—and a determined seeking after freer forms of community life, within which man's existence can be less fettered and more satisfying.

The story, of course, is not a new one, but the elements in it are more appreciated today than ever they were before. Since Toennies wrote his classic work on "community" (*Gemeinschaft*) and "institution" (*Gesellschaft*), there has been a growing realization on the part of social scientists of the importance of balancing these correlative aspects of human society. For every society is both "community" and "institution" and it is of the utmost importance that neither aspect overcome the other. On the one hand, it is a community of people, that is, an informal grouping, personal or rather interpersonal in character, unorganized without being disorganized, unstructured, democratic and spontaneous in its activities, charismatic—to use a piece of latter-day jargon—in short, an association of free men. On the other hand, every society is also an institution or at least has an institutional aspect. This in turn can be described in many ways. It is the formal, impersonal, structured aspect of society, society as organized and legalized by authority which, if overdone, can cause it to be strait-jacketted and totalitarian.

The social problem *par excellence* has always been the effecting of a balance between the community and institutional aspects of society. Overemphasis of the one at the expense of the other is certain to cause dissatisfaction and restlessness. To stress the aspect of community, without remembering that of institution, is to set in motion a process which will culminate in anarchy. Likewise to stress institution, while forgetting community, is to launch a development which must end in authoritarianism. Society is healthy and truly human only when it combines due elements of both community and institution. Aquinas as a social philosopher was well aware of this and wrote about it in his *De Regimine Principum*:

> If it is natural to man that he live in the society of many, it is necessary that there be some agency by which the grouping be ruled. For with each one tending to follow his own inclinations, the grouping would disperse into diverse fragments, unless there were some agency which looked after the common good of all (*Bk. I*, ch. 1).

There has always been tension between community and institution; it is far from easy to achieve a proper balance of these social ingredients. The history of the Church and of society in general is full of examples of failure to do so. At one period there has been too much emphasis on community, at another on institution. In the domain of secular society take for example the history of the university. It was not today nor yesterday that a movement for the abolition of "structures" first appeared in the context of universities. As early as the thirteenth century, resentment against authority in the University of Paris was so keenly felt as to produce the radical dissenters known as the Goliards. In very many ways they remind us of the radical students of today. Homer Haskins has described them vividly in his *The Rise of Universities* (New York, 1923). They were, he says, an order of vagrants

> open to men of every condition and every clime, with its rules which are no rules, late-risers, gamesters, roysterers, proud that none of its members has more than one coat to his back . . . . . Often bibulous and erotic, the Goliardic verse contains a large amount of parody and satire. Appealing to a public familiar with scripture and liturgy, its authors parody everything—the Bible, hymns to the Virgin, the canon of the Mass, as in the "Drinkers Mass" . . . . . One of the best known pieces is a satire on the Papacy under the caption of "The Gospel according to Marks of Silver". This is only one of many bitter attacks on Rome, while the pride, hardness and greed of the higher clergy are portrayed in "Golias the Bishop".

It is not surprising that an element like this should have so disrupted university life as to make it necessary to introduce stern measures to support authority. In this connection it is significant, although little known, that the first introduction of the police to the Sorbonne was as early as 1229, when they were brought in at the request of the king, leading to student riots which did not ease off until 1231 (cf. Jacques le Goff, *Les Intellectuels au Moyen Age*, Paris, 1965). In the heel of the hunt, the institutional element was victorious to an extent that can only be regarded as exaggerated. Readers of Helen Waddell's *The Wandering Scholars* (London, 1952) know the kind of strictures that came to be imposed on students of the Goliardic type.

In the Church the swing of the pendulum has also tended to move from too great an emphasis on institution to that on community, or vice versa as the case may be. There can be little doubt that, from the sociological standpoint, the Protestant Reformation was a reaction against the institutional Church of the Middle Ages. It is true, of course, that many factors went into its making, purely historical and theological as well as sociological. But without the appropriate predisposing sociological conditions, it could never have had the success which attended it. Certainly anyone who believes that this success was due chiefly to the scholarship of a Luther or the spirituality of a Henry VIII is missing the wood for the trees. What these men did was to assume leadership of an already existing and inexorable movement—a movement by way of reaction to the over institutional, over authoritative, over clerical Church of the medieval period. It is noticeable how, in one way or another, all forms of Protestanism tended to delimit clerical authority in the Church. Some forms, like Anglicanism, did so only to a modified degree, others, like Quakerism, to such a degree as to altogether eliminate the sacerdotal ministry. Indeed some sects so deinstitutionalized the Church as to foster a religious community without any formal structures. The cure proved as unacceptable as the disease, leading to an extreme of anarchical individualism. So much so, in fact, that the Quakers were forced to seek new forms of institution, in place of authority, if their community was not to disintegrate totally. Maps, with the location of Quaker families entered in and a schedule of inter-familial visitation attached, have come down to us from eighteenth century England. They represent a novel, cartographic, type of social institution whereby the unity and cohesion of the community could be maintained in the absence of authority and law.

The perennial difficulty of achieving a satisfactory balance between the community and institutional aspects of society is heavily aggravated by the mass character of contemporary life in the urban-industrial world. For mass society and mass culture, by the very conditions of their existence, are subject to an extremely high degree of institutionalization. Precisely because it is mass society, the urban-industrial world of today tends to generate structures almost to the point of suffocating human community. Whyte in his *Organization Man* (New York, 1956) and Marcuse in his *One Dimensional Man* (Boston, 1964) have given us an analysis of how circumscribed human liberty can become when social structures are too multiple and too complex.

This is something that keen thinkers have long been aware of; the difference in today's situation is that its truth is more easily recognizable. In the year 1800 America was a long way from megalopolis, yet Jefferson could even then say that he viewed great cities "as pestilential to the . . . . liberties of men" (Cf. M. and L. White, *The Intellectual versus the City*, Massachusetts, 1962). Later in the century, Emerson declared that city people "live for show, servile to public opinion". What they meant was that urban living, at least in the larger centres, tends to catch people up and absorb them into the environment, an environment in which their choices, while many, are

so institutionalized as to lack some of the more important
elements of real freedom. Life, as one acute English ob-
server has put it, becomes to a high degree a matter of
"Keeping Up With the Joneses" (Cf. Lee Gibb, *The
Joneses*, London, 1959). Willy nilly one finds oneself
a victim of the "rat race", conforming to an established
pattern of affluent living or endeavouring with might
and main to attain to it. It was this kind of thing that
Thorsten Veblen had in mind when, in 1899, he penned
his *Theory of the Leisure Class*. In this he underlined
the pattern of conspicuous consumption of the city dwel-
ler. By and large people can judge one another's position
in urban society only by way of the goods they display.

This is particularly true of capitalist society, the core
of the urban-industrial world. Within it the life of man
becomes to a frightening degree geared to the production
and consumption of material things. One produces more
and more, to consume more and more, and to go on
doing the same thing over and over again within the
terms dictated by the needs of an expanding economy.
An economy that is ironically called a "free" economy,
for it tends to generate a society that is anything but
free in the full and true sense of the term. So much so
that John Galbraith in *The New Industrial State* (Boston,
1967) sees many affinities between developed capitalist
and socialist society as far as their impact on the life of
the person is concerned. It takes the French to produce
short and descriptive phrases to cover complicated entities
and developments. In face of the present-day capitalist
phenomenon which we are dealing with here they have
given us the apt phrase *"Societé de Consommation"*.

A vast amount is summed up by this—a society that is
dominated by the pull of persuasion far beyond the limits
of legitimate advertisement, a society that to a high degree is not based on real needs but which subordinates
the life of the individual to the business of catering for

11

these needs and to the extent of practically enslaving him within it. Prone to feel the pressure of what others think he should do, hyper-sensitive to the meaning and importance of promotion, men tend to live their lives in a mesh of established patterns that inhibit their freedom at every hand's turn. Even their leisure itself tends to be structured, as even brief experience of the quality of living in a very large city will show. It is quite true that, over against his rural grandfather, the city man of today has a wide variety of choices as to how to use his leisure. He has a car; there is cinema and television; one can do things and go places hitherto undreamed of. And yet, when all is said and done, what a grey pattern of sameness is there to be discerned in the leisure habits of modern urban man. The very density of his environmental circumstances almost dictate this. He is lucky if, on a summer Sunday, traffic conditions permit him to take the family out to the beach. Lucky too if the demand for ice-cream on the beach is not so great as to discourage him from joining the queue. Of course he can always stay at home and watch television! But on the morrow he will be up and about early to begin a new week of consolidation of the system. Is he a free man? Of course he is—in a way. But in another way he is a kind of impersonal product, a pawn in the workings of society. It was this, I imagine, which Lloyd Wright had in mind when, at the end of *The Living City* (New York, 1958), he quoted Emerson to the effect that "cities force growth and make men talkative and entertaining, but they make them artificial".

The basic reason for it all is that our urban-industrial society is immensely more "institutional" than "community" orientated. In Toennies's terminology, its characteristic is *Gesellschaft*; it is and it has to be highly organized. Even a moment's reflection yields a host of examples of institutional forms or structures in the big city. Living accommodation is organized in skyscraper buildings, the means of transportation in subways and flyovers. In economic life one finds the appearance of the supermarket, in the diffusion of information the press, television and radio, in the field of entertainment the theatre and cinema, and in the domain of religion the erection of vast parishes and churches. Nor should we be mistaken about the need for these structures; mass society simply could not do without them. They are at once the products and the necessary supports of the technological society of our day. Anything less than mass society could not make possible the advanced technology necessary to produce them. At the same time, this society itself could not exist without the organizational infrastructure which they afford.

The unfortunate thing is that, as institutions, they involve relationships between individuals rather than between persons. They are created, rather than living, personal bonds. And because of this, urban-industrial society may be said to subsist primarily on impersonal structures. To a considerable degree it lacks—or rather tends to lack—*Gemeinschaft*, the community life of the family and the locality, of the village, the smaller town, the owner-operated shop, the rural church. It finds it harder by far than do these latter primary groupings to afford the possibility of the face-to-face relationships that are normally necessary for real interpersonal exchange. In this connection one has only to contrast the entire field of experience as between buying in a small shop and in a city supermarket. One should, of course, avoid exaggeration. In their own way, city blocks and suburban neighbourhoods can give rise to their own forms of interpersonal relations and community. My point is that it is increasingly difficult for them to do so. In its own way too, small-scale society can absorb some of the structures of city society without suffering any great change in the process. One can find supermarkets of a kind even in villages. The point here, however, is that, while this is so, such city-type organizational forms are accidental to the small society whereas they are essential to the big society from which they overspill. It is equally true that if the big society is sufficiently big, one can sometimes find face-to-face relationships within it without the normal consequence, the emergence of community. Not so long ago the *Sunday Times* described how this takes place in the context of a London commuters' train. Every morning the same people come across one another, come to know where each gets on and off, what newspapers or magazines each reads, what ailments each is heir to— yet without ever breaking the anonymity of the one to the other as far as personal relationships are concerned.

It is the anonymity and impersonal nature of urban-industrial society that disposes men to being rather passive and artificial. Which in turn makes it much more difficult for them to develop a true sense of loyalty. How discerning the American philosopher Josiah Royce was when, in his *Philosophy of Loyalty* published in 1908, he spoke about the "self-estranged spirit" of city living—with its over centralized agencies of government and overwhelming commercial power, its multitudinous and crushing structures of all kinds. These things, said Royce, do not permit an opportunity "for such loyalty as our distinctively provincial fathers used to express in their early utterances of the national spirit . . . . . They excite our loyalty as little as do the trade winds or the blizzard. They leave our patriotic sentiments cold. The smoke of our civilization hides the very heavens that used to be so near".

As the twentieth century has progressed we see more clearly the perspicacity of Royce's insights. Both society in general and the Church afford examples of what he had in mind. To take one instance, one remembers the relatively easy defection of American G.I.'s in North Korean prisoner of war camps, as contrasted with the tenacity of the rural Turks—something which Eugene Kinkead in his interesting book *In Every War But One* (New York, 1959) attributes to the kinds of society which had fashioned the respective groups. And speaking of this matter, one wonders whether the current anti-war attitudes of American youth are entirely due to a moral conviction of the illegitimacy of the American presence in Vietnam or whether they may not also, and perhaps mainly, spring from a disinterest in national affairs as such. One cannot be loyal just to structures and institutions; one cannot die for skyscrapers and subways, fly-overs and supermarkets. One can be loyal only to people, to persons in a community, to a human fabric which one knows in a human way. It is for this reason that totalitarian States everywhere have always been inimical to the smaller and voluntary societies. For they cannot brook competition with their own omnicompetent designs and they know full well how much easier it is for the smaller society to command the loyalty of its members than for the larger. Hence the crushing by Hitler's Germany of trade unions, religious youth bodies and the like.

It is for the same reason that it is so difficult for the Church in the urban-industrial framework to command the loyalty even of the practising. For in this same context the Church finds itself hemmed in, as it were, by the needs of a highly institutionalized religious life. One thinks, for instance, of the gigantic parishes and huge church buildings which have become a regular feature of religion in the city. The Church has a very definite human side to it and it exists in the human society of its day. As a result it is saddled with the same disadvantages as are part and parcel of its secular social *milieu*. In the urban-industrial *milieu* its members experience the same self-estrangement as we have spoken of earlier, when

155

compelled to worship in the institution—represented by vast parishes and vast Church buildings—rather than in community orientated structures. It is no argument to point to the huge cathedrals that were a commonplace of medieval towns. For a cathedral is a special kind of church, a focal point for diocesan liturgical activity, a necessary centre of religious unity. Yet it is significant that, in medieval times, the cathedrals were used mainly for the celebration of special events with pomp and pageantry. The day to day life of religion, even in the cathedral towns, was carried on in the smaller churches which also abounded. Not so in the Church as organized in the modern urban-industrial world. Nor do the problems of the Church, which spring from the spirit of this society, by any manner of means stop here. On the contrary, one gets the impression that one of the chief pivots of difficulty in the contemporary Church is precisely that of a Church establishment which is so highly organized as to have lost the sense of true community. One feels this almost palpably in the American scene when confronted with an episcopal conference of over two hundred members. And this is but one out of a hundred possible examples of how large-scale society affects life within the Church.

The "self-estrangement" of the person in contemporary society is only a step from what psychologists call "alienation"—alienation with its correlative patterns of deviant behaviour, whether on the part of isolated individuals or of groups. Indeed alienation of one kind or another might be said to be such a widespread phenomenon of society today as to constitute *the* condition of contemporary Western man and particularly of Western youth. There is a neurotic striving to escape the structures which will otherwise absorb youth, mould them into what they see as the slavish lives of their fathers, make them tools of the *societé de consommation*. Hence their patent unrest.

In the non-ecclesial domain, contemporary patterns of protest have by now led some to open revolt against the establishment and to a determined effort to build a new and better world. Since the 1950s the "Angry Young Men" and the "Protest Generation" have been coming to attract more and more attention. Whether as the British "beatniks", the Dutch "provos" or the American "hippies", they have come to personify the revolt against contemporary society. In their extremism they are anti-everything—against the government, the police, the employers, university administration and the Church. *Graffiti* all over Paris after *les jours de Mai 1968* summed it all up in the phrase *Ni Dieu ni maitre*. These are the "outsiders" of the latter-day world, as the Goliards were in the world of their day and the early Christians in that of the pagan Roman Empire. To say that the hippies are like the Christians in this respect is not at all to imply that they are the same in every respect. Without any doubt many hippies overdo it and become the victims of dirt and drug addiction, to say nothing of idleness and promiscuity. In truth they would be saints if they did not, for man is a social animal and to drop out from society, for whatever reason, supposes either superhuman courage or despair. And many of these people do despair —of society as they know it and of its reform. For these it is all too easy to turn to drugs, as men earlier did to drink when it was cheaper than drugs. Free love, needless to say, costs nothing. As for cleanliness, it can easily become a fetish, *a va sans dire* of a chromium-plated society. In this one respect perhaps, beyond all the others, the early Christian hermits are likely to have been least different from the hippies. The St. Jerome of El Greco, as a Renaissance prelate, has little in common with the more credible Jerome of the School of Rembrandt, the long-haired, cave-dwelling anchorite. Nor is it clear how Simon Stylites took a bath. In any case there are hippies and hippies; there are many miles of difference between San Francisco's Haight Ashbury and at least some of the communes of Northern California. Yet it is amazing how many presumably intelligent people cannot see this or are so worshipful of the sacred cow of American society as to refuse to believe that anybody can be so alienated by it as to drop out and still remain within the ambit of the decent life.

The fact is that this can and does happen. Just at the moment there are many people who have opted out in order to search for a more congenial world. As always the extreme examples get the publicity. Jack Kerouac was one of the best-known of the early post-war searchers, entirely typified by his novel *On the Road* (New York, 1958). More recent searchers have used music more than writing as a medium for the expression of their ideas. Such was the Beatle hit of 1967, entitled *She's leaving home*. Such also the Seekers' number *A World of our own*: "We will build a world of our own that no one else can share; All our troubles we will leave far behind us there; And I know what you will find there will be peace of mind there; When we live in a world of our own". One cannot refrain from remembering Yeats's *Innisfree*: "I will arise and go now and go to Innisfree; And a small cabin build there of clay and wattle made . . . . . And I shall have some peace there for peace comes dropping slow . . . . . "

Such sanctuaries are hard to find, in the modern world even more than before. Yeats's *Innisfree* had no real existence, no more than the havens of refuge of the majority of contemporary "outsiders" who have to make do with a world of fantasy like that of Kerouac's *The Subterraneans* or the Beatles' escape *The Yellow Submarine*. But whether its location be underwater or underground, it is always a new and different world from that of the present. A few try the more difficult and demanding expedient of building a personal world in the rural communes.

But their's is just the more extreme and publicized reaction to a situation which is coterminous with society. The university scene provides another example of revolt against structures that are seen as extinguishing the life of the person. Marshall McLuhan has written extensively of why the "teach-in" and "sit-in" accompany the "drop-out" in the university setting:

There is a world of difference between the modern home environment of integrated electric information and the classroom. Today's television child is attuned to up-to-the-minute "adult" news—inflation, rioting, war, taxes, crime, bathing beauties—and is bewildered when he enters the nineteenth century environment that still characterizes the educational establishment where information is scarce but ordered and structured by fragmented, classified patterns, subjects and schedules. It is naturally an environment much like any factory set-up with its inventories and assembly lines . . . . . Many of our institutions suppress all the natural direct experience of youth . . . . . The student finds no means of involvement for himself and cannot discover how the educational scheme relates to his mythic world of electronically processed data and experience that his clear and direct responses report . . . . . We now experience simultaneously the drop-out and the teach-in. The two forms are correlative. They belong together. The teach-in represents an attempt to shift education from instruction to discovery, from brainwashing students to brainwashing instructors. It is a big, dramatic reversal. Vietnam, as the content of the teach-in, is a very small and perhaps misleading Red Herring. It really has little to do with the teach-in, as such, anymore than with the drop-out.

The drop-out represents a rejection of nineteenth century technology as manifested in our educational establishments. The teach-in represents a creative effort, switching the educational effort from package to discovery. (*The Medium is the Message,* New York, 1967, pp. 18, 100 and 101).

In the Church there is discernible a similar development, of which the current emphasis on freedom of conscience is a manifestation. Oftentimes it carries with it bizarre forms of behaviour and a general independence *vis-à-vis* authority. Cleric as well as layman has become caught up in it, as witness the example of Fathers Camillo Torres in revolutionary politics, Kilsdonk on the issue of celibacy, Dubay and Groppi on the question of Negro rights, Berrigan on the Vietnam draft, and Davis and Shannon in the matter of birth control. Some such protestors have already begun to crystallize around a structural nucleus—"The Underground Church". Further examples of the same thing are the appearance of spontaneous worship-groups like the "Free Church" at Berkeley, California. For it is a curious irony that, by reason of the social nature of man and his need for a measure of institutionalization, even revolt againt institutions itself tends to become institutionalized and rejected structures replaced by new ones.

It was in virtue of this process that the Non-Conformist groupings of the Reformation era evolved quickly from "sects" to "churches". It is ironical in that the very people whose revolt was anti-structure should themselves have become structured relatively quickly. The same thing is true of the contemporary freedom seekers. One becomes unfree to be anything other than a revolutionary; there is no option but to be "with it" in rejecting social pressures; liberty extends to nothing that is not liberal. So marked in fact has this phenomenon become among

160

the anti-establishment sector of latter-day youth—by whom, in order to be accepted, one has to wear way-out garb, take drugs and indulge in sexual promiscuity—that a couple of years ago a number of American hippies solemnly interred their movement and replaced it with what was known as "The Freebies". As a freebie one would be free to do as one liked—take drugs or not take drugs, be promiscuous or not be promiscuous, don bizzare attire or not don it, etc. It is in search of the same freedom that groups of hippies from San Francisco have been fleeing from the "anarchical pressures" of Haight-Ashbury and trying to find real liberty and peace in the Sierras. So much so that 1969 became known as "The Year of the Commune" (Cf. *Life* magazine, August, 1969). And yet, such is man's need for some measure of institutionalization that even the communes are finding it necessary to introduce it at least surreptitiously. Perhaps unconsciously would be a better way of putting it. During the Summer of 1969 considerable publicity was given to an episode which occurred in one of them when a small boy, falling before the blandishments of the consumer society, slipped away from the commune to acquire and eat a candy bar. Reprimand for the "crime", which would not be allowed to pass unnoticed, took the form of a "laugh-in" or collective derision towards the little fellow. The interesting thing is that this very practice is found among certain primitive societies who have not yet developed an elaborate system of law and order. Thus can the reaction to secular structures end up in a rigid enough system of new structures.

The Church in its turn must also be careful that over-regimentation does not breed a reaction in favour of a liberalism that itself will become strait-jacketted. Sometime ago I remember coming across a report in some French Catholic magazine which told of the brusque action of a "progressive" country curé who ejected from his church three old ladies, whose wont it had been for over thirty years to tell their beads there every day. His grounds for doing so were that such unliturgical devotions were no longer to be encouraged. No wonder the title of the French comprehensive account of this kind of liberal dictatorship in the Church, is the rather startling one *Le Terreur Progressiste* (Paris, 1969).

What, one may ask, is to be our approach if it is not a middle of the road course between extremes? No other reasonable alternative is open to us. The extremes in themselves lead to trouble. One has got to try to steer a way between the individualism of the liberal *élite* and the traditionalism of the mass of the people, between the democratic community freedom that is an essential prerequisite of progress and the social structures that are needed for stability.

Today's choice, whether in society in general, the university or the Church, simply cannot be allowed to be a choice between *anarchism* and *authoritarianism*. It is essential that a *tertium quid* be found.

Now is the time to endeavour to strike a balance, for there are indications to the effect that, if this is not done, there is likely to be a sharp and unhealthy reaction to contemporary permissiveness. This is already evident in secular society where an incipient puritanism is beginning to rear its far from handsome head. I am thinking, for example, of the American Purity League about which *Time* reported some time ago, and which has overtones of an undesirable anti-sex crusade. An analogous development in face of the excessive student "freedom-fighting" in the universities is the proposal to introduce Federal legislation to secure the forceful control of American campuses.

Something similar could happen in the Church—and it would be nothing short of disastrous. If an exaggerated emphasis on freedom of conscience led to a conscientious licence, this in turn could cause a reaction in favour of a renewed authoritarianism that, if anything, would be likely to be more pronounced that anything hitherto seen. It would in fact be a disfiguration of Christianity.

11

Minority and Majority Rights

PERHAPS THE most difficult area in which a balance between liberty and order, community and society, conscience and law can be effected is that in which conflict exists between minority and majority rights. The unfortunate thing is that this situation all too often prevails, especially as regards matters moral and religious. At the time of writing, for example, one can find plenty of instances of this. The question of liberalizing the divorce laws in Canada and the introduction of divorce in Italy, the abortion law in Britain, the issues of divorce and contraception in Ireland—all of these matters and many others of a like nature hinge strongly on the meeting point between the rights of conscience of minorities and majorities in these countries.

The Republic of Ireland provides probably the best framework for a discussion of this problem because of its history and the size of its Catholic population. And for some time now there have been indications that the problem is coming to the fore, as articulate minorities begin a forceful push for the introduction of a number of legislative changes that on the face of it at least would seem inappropriate in a heavily Catholic country.

Basic to all this is the question of revising the Irish Constitution, which underpins the country's entire legal structure. Already a Report has come out from a Governmental Committee set up to examine into its feasibility. More recently, and on more than one occasion, the head of the Government, Mr. Lynch, has also indicated that far-reaching changes in the juridical domain are possible and may be necessary if the Catholic South is ever to unite with the North of Ireland. The area of divorce is one of those instanced. All this has set off a debate about the propriety of what is called "a secular law" for a predominantly "Catholic country" such as Ireland.

Quite a number of people would certainly regard it as quite inappropriate and unacceptable to traditional Irish life. On the other hand, there is a point of view coming increasingly to be expressed to the effect that it is facile to describe contemporary Ireland simply as a Catholic country and that, in any case, considerations relating to the area of "private morality" have nothing to do with the problem.

One writer has put this as follows in the context of divorce:

> The whole question of whether or not Catholics should be allowed divorce in certain circumstances is one which will continue to fascinate Catholic exegetes and Catholic moral theologians for generations to come. But there is no reason why it should continue to fascinate, in the same way, the elected representatives of the people of this country (John Horgan, "Towards a Secular Law, *The Irish Times*, 2 March, 1971).

He adds:

> The basic issue is whether or not we are capable of framing a decent secular constitution for this country

which will guarantee freedom of conscience, and avoid the fallacy of temporizing interminably between the claims of a possibly infinite number of ecclesiastical establishments.

To say all this is not by any means to argue that Irish Christians should be indifferent to all forms of social legislation. It is to argue that a society's laws are not necessarily an accurate guide to its moral standards; that there is an important (and in Ireland unacknowledged) distinction to be made between any particular set of moral standards and legal rights; and that unthinking reliance by Christians on civil law to enforce their own moral insights is at best a half-hearted and fearful response to the challenge implicit in their faith.

The question of contraceptives has drawn similar views from other quarters. Thus the Irish Family Planning Rights Association has declared that it "seeks the democratic right for all parents to freely and responsibly plan their families, in the manner best suited to their consciences and circumstances. We declare that the State has no right whatever in legislating in this internal family area, and we seek to change the present unjust prohibition of knowledge and means for responsible family planning" (*The Irish Times*, 6 March, 1971).

And finally the view of a letter-writer to a newspaper:

Like divorce, it is quite irrelevant whether contraceptives are considered good or bad by the majority of people. If they are wanted or needed by any sort of minority who can see no crime in using them, they should be there for the asking. I fail to see why any "democratic majority" should have a say in some-

166

thing which does not affect it (*The Irish Times*, 10 March, 1971).

Against this background, it is not surprising to find proposals made to introduce a more modified law on contraceptives. This in itself has raised a further and complicated issue regarding what attitude should be taken by political parties to such moral matters. The political correspondent for one newspaper put it rather curiously when he wrote that, on such an issue, it was almost certain that all the parties would allow their members a "free vote", which would enable them "to vote according to their consciences" (*The Sunday Press*, 7 March, 1971).

To cap the matter, the Irish Minister for Foreign Affairs has given formal expression to the view that law reform may be necessary in the interests of liberal stances for the general good. The Irish, he said, should not continue to cling to the notion that fundamental, statutory or other law, including the Constitution, should express confessional or paternalistic attitudes. The following paragraphs contain the essence of his thought:

> This might make it necessary for us to distinguish between our duties in our capacity as legislators and our personal beliefs about private behaviour. Bearing in mind that individual freedom to decide on matters of private morality did not impose a standard of behaviour on anyone else, the legislature was certainly not bound to express prohibitions in matters which adult people felt entitled to decide for themselves.
>
> To put it bluntly, in a plural society, legislators must guard against considering matters solely from the standpoint of their personal religious practices. They had no duty to do so. Indeed it could well become impossible in a plural society to obtain general agreement to social legislation—and such general

12

agreement was the cement that bound society together—if legislative matters affecting private morality were to be decided only on the basis of the private conscience of the legislators (*The Irish Times,* 10 March, 1971).

To examine this matter fully would take a great deal more space than I have at my disposal here. Even a cursory examination of the few pieces that I have quoted above gives ample evidence of a need for clarification. One wonders, for example, whether it is not the custom of the representatives of the people to vote always "according to their consciences"? One wonder too, if these same representatives should not be fascinated "in the same way" as moral theologians with moral issues, why they should not be fascinated by them for other reasons, such as political? And one also wonders what kind of logic could suggest that if any particular moral stand is "needed by any sort of minority" it should "be there for the asking"—even if considered bad by the majority of the people—on the grounds that it is hard to see how any "democratic majority should have a say in something which does not affect it".

Which raises the deeper question as to what exactly is meant by "private morality" and how to decide whether something in this area is so private that it can in no way affect the general interest or that of the majority. What is called the "internal family area" is in the same category—as the laws against bigamy attest. In this connection too, it might at least be surmised that it is possible that the general interest can sometimes be served—albeit indirectly—by some curbs on "individual freedom to decide on matters of private morality", even when this freedom does not "impose a standard of behaviour on anyone else". The public weal, one may suspect, can be injured by private behaviour in many ways other than this. Lastly, one is forced to examine the precise meaning of "a plural society" and its implications for legislators from the point of view of their social duty, when there are issues before them on which their "personal religious practices" impinge.

Towards an analysis of such matters one can scarcely do better than probe more deeply the proposal to legalize divorce in the Republic of Ireland.

It is now nearly four years since the publication of the Report on the Constitution. In the intervening period a number of its recommendations—and notably that concerning divorce—have come to be seen as of less pressing practical import than appeared when they were first suggested. Once raised, however, such issues continue to present an intellectual challenge which will remain until they are adequately dealt with.

In so far as it is a real issue, the question boils down to whether jurisdiction for divorce on statutory grounds should be introduced in the interest of that small minority —irrespective of religious affiliation—who for one reason or another may feel this desirable. And my purpose here is to try to provide a response to this question that will be in harmony with basic Catholic principles.

As far as the law of Christ is concerned—that is, the moral law for Christians as found in the pages of the New Testament—while there have been differences of interpretation among the different Churches and today even some differences of opinion among Catholic theologians themselves, it has been and continues to be the official teaching of the Church that it was the intention of Christ (as found, for example, in St. Matthew's Gospel, chapter 19, verses 3-12) to exclude the practice of divorce among his followers. In other words, divorce is contrary to the law of God, in the sense of the moral law as revealed by Christ.

What, however, of the law of God, in the sense of the natural law? Here the position is more hotly disputed. The more commonly accepted, more traditional, view of ethicians has been that divorce is entirely contrary to the natural law. These ethicians have argued that divorce is excluded by reason, because it is inimical to the attainment not only of the secondary but of even the primary ends of marriage in so far as these include the rearing of children.

For some time now it is being realized that this is not so, or at least, that it is not necessarily so in all cases. There is the hard fact also that divorce can scarcely be absolutely contrary to natural law seeing that it was allowed by God himself in the Old Testament (Deut. Ch. 24, v. 1 seq.). For these reasons a second, more moderate view of the matter has been adopted by a number of ethicians. According to these, divorce, while it is out of harmony with what reason suggests is generally the better arrangement for marriage, is not strictly contrary to the natural law in circumstances in which its permission is not clearly opposed to either the primary or the secondary ends of marriage.

This view has received considerable backing from the studies of anthropologists, who have demonstrated the widespread existence of divorce as an institution in societies not specifically Christian. For it has long been recognized that the universal or quasi-universal practice of mankind constitutes a secondary and manifestative criterion of natural law morality. Hence it is that a growing number of ethicians are beginning to take the view that, in circumstances in which the ends of a marriage cannot be properly attained, divorce—under the control of properly constituted authority—can be licit, at least as far as the natural law is concerned. In other words, it is not absolutely contrary to the law of God, in the sense of the moral law as discovered by reason.

It is interesting to note that, except for some extremely primitive societies, divorce is carefully regulated by social authority and can only be had with its consent. Even in those instances in which this is not clearly seen to hold, the adoption of an adequate cross-cultural perspective will usually show that the institution is surrounded by very real, even if not too obvious, community norms. This is not surprising in view of the relevance of family stability for society of every kind. For which reason, in developed societies, State authority is the premier candidate for the right to regulate the granting of divorce.

This, I am sure, is what Father Fergal O'Connor, the Irish Dominican, had in mind, when in an interview accorded to a newspaper he stated categorically that, as far as the abstract principles of public morality are concerned, there are circumstances in which the State can introduce divorce legislation. In view of what has been said concerning the law of Christ, however, it should be clear that divorce is still contrary to the law of God in this sense and that it is therefore unlawful for Christians, who believe in and are bound by the law of Christ, to avail themselves of a State provision which allows divorce.

It is with the natural law that the State is primarily concerned. In particular, it is of concern to the State to be able to establish whether or not the introduction or permission of any institution is consistent with the common temporal good of the community. Because of this, it is of paramount importance to establish whether the introduction of legislation permitting divorce would inevitably open the flood gates to abuse of the institution, in a way that could undermine the stability of the family and injure society.

There is no denying that wherever divorce has once been introduced, it has become so widespread as to constitute a grave social evil. Britain and the United States are cases in point. In the latter country, whereas in 1887 there was one divorce for every seventeen marriages, by 1945 the proportion was one in three (1,612,992 marriages, 485,000 divorces). The growth of the divorce rate has been similar in Britain, causing successive Royal Commissions on Population to call for some method of stemming its increase.

The reason for the spread of divorce has, of course, been abuse of the system, as the legal history of divorce proves clearly. A situation quickly develops in which either the grave reasons usually required for divorce become broadened in practice by lax interpretations, or else, while grave reasons must exist both in theory and in practice, they are artificially produced by way of collusion between the parties. So much so that recently in Britain, the proposal was pressed in certain quarters that a better situation would emerge if the grounds for divorce were changed to simple proof that a marriage had broken down. But here again there are many snags. Will the adoption of the proposal mean virtually the introduction of divorce by consent? Will it mean also that only the wealthy will be enabled to enjoy whatever benefits it confers, since financial provision for the legal process as well as for wife and children has got to be made? Or, will this latter aspect be eventually attended to by the Welfare State, after the manner of free legal aid and children's allowances? If so, what social evils will not ensue? Indeed some commentators have gone so far as to maintain that *such* a weakening of marriage and the family would result, as to constitute a social crisis of the first magnitude.

In somewhat the same way, the abortion law in Britain is coming in for some hard-hitting criticism. As Norman St. John Stevas, Conservative M.P., has put it:

> The abuses that have arisen under the Act are too well known to detail: the legalized rackets operated by unscrupulous doctors, the lack of after-care in private clinics, the unsavoury practices centering around foreign women at London Airport have received wide publicity" (*Sunday Press*, 7 March, 1971).

There is a difference of course between the character of peoples and one cannot immediately jump to the conclusion that the introduction of divorce legislation in Ireland would inevitably lead to a situation such as exists in Britain. It might be hoped that a situation could be arrived at in which divorce would be allowed in the interests of a small minority who wanted it, while at the same time it would be so hedged round with carefully applied regulations that there would be no danger of its being abused to the detriment of the community as a whole. This is undoubtedly the situation which the Report on the Constitution wished to bring into being. It is also the situation theoretically referred to by those who point out that the State must, at one and the same time, both respect the individual consciences of its citizens and take account of the beliefs and traditions of the community for which it is legislating.

The big question to be answered is, whether respect for the rights of conscience on the part of a minority which wants divorce, is capable of coexisting side by side with respect for a majority attitude to marriage and the family, according to which divorce constitutes an unacceptable social value. In other words, the question is whether a system can be worked out in which divorce is allowed, so as to respect the values of the individual conscience which demands it, while at the same time respecting the social values of the community as a whole, for which the permission of divorce represents an unacceptable moral standard.

A purely empirical answer to this problem is not sufficient. It simply is not enough to say that a solution might be arrived at by a careful survey of the effect which the introduction of divorce would have on the morals of a society, its social consequences for marriage and the family and indeed the entire structure of the society as a whole. It is true that these considerations are relevant to the problem but a weighing up of them is insufficient in itself and, if pursued to the neglect of more basic considerations, would in effect be a refusal to face the real question.

This latter is at rock-bottom the question of a balancing of rights, the principles concerning which cannot be given due attention by any exclusive weighing of empirical evidence. This indeed was recognized by the Chairman of the Committee on the Constitution, when in the course of an interview he said:

> The basic thought, I think, that was in the minds of the members of the Committee was this, that if any reputable recognized Church in this country has tenets which don't interfere with the rights of people of other churches, it is wrong and contrary to religious freedom that we should have in our Constitution a provision which prohibits them from operating on the basis of the tenets of their religion.

There you have the centre of the divorce problem—whether respect for the rights of a minority who believe in divorce does, or does not, interfere with the rights of the majority who do not. It should be said at once that, in the case of the majority, there is more to the matter than not interfering with their right as individuals not to practise divorce. There is question in addition of not interfering with their rights as members of the community. These rights demand respect for the social values which are reflected in the general politico-legal framework of life in the society which as majority they have exercized themselves in constructing. And they are rights which can be interfered with, not only by outright denial or withdrawal, but by indirect influence which tends to undermine them.

Of course the basic problem for democracy has always been this—the achievement of a nice balance between rights, whether individual or social, and the protection of as many rights as possible from interference, whether direct or indirect. This, in truth, is the function of law. As such, it is its primary interest to look to the good of the community as a whole rather than to directly seek the good of individuals or of minorities. Indeed, there are times when the achievement of the common good of the community entails a refusal of some good sought by a section. These are the hard facts of political life as practised even in a democratic context. We should not be so unrealistic as to build up claims on the part of individuals or minorities who represent dissenting values—even in matters of conscience—such as would lead to the imposition of their standards rather than the standards of the majority, in the field of social values. People are generally free to choose the community to which they will belong, and there will always be some who are prepared to change their allegiance from one community to another for reasons of climate, or taxation, or housing standards—to say nothing of basic disagreement with social values.

In a society in which the great majority of the people prefer a social fabric in which divorce is not recognized, to introduce it in the name of a minority seems extremely close to legislating directly for the good of the part. It is true that the argument could be advanced that such provision is also for the good of the whole. After all, it is along these lines that State provision for such things as an institute for advanced studies can properly be made. Thus it could be said that just as it is in the interest of society as a whole that adequate facilities for air-sea rescue be available to succour those cases of hardship which call for it, so also it is right and proper that the State should come to the rescue of those hard cases who unfortunately need facilities for divorce. To do so, it could be argued, is no more than to show a delicate appreciation for their conscientious rights, something that is entirely proper in circumstances in which it is clear that no ill consequences will follow for society as a whole.

Forceful though the foregoing argument may seem, there is one consequence to which it pays insufficient attention. This is the fact that, as a matter of history, divorce legislation and secularization have gone hand in hand. This is evident in both Catholic and Protestant countries. In France it was first introduced in 1792, in the immediate wake of the rationalism of the Revolution. In Portugal and elsewhere, during the nineteenth century, it came into the picture under the aegis of so-called liberal but anti-religious regimes. In Britain too it first emerged in the growing secular climate of the last century. Despite his reputation, Henry VIII did not introduce divorce. His many changes of wives were effected, either by claiming the nullity of marriage or by way of the convenient death of a partner followed by remarriage. Under Elizabeth too the marriage laws of England remained entirely Catholic in this respect. The most that was allowed was separation, on a promise not to remarry. And this remained the position up to the nineteenth century, except for a few divorces by way of Private Bills of Parliament. The setting up of the Divorce Court in 1857 represented the decline of English society in the direction of an unchristian and amoral secularism, a decline which, regrettably, seems to have been followed by the Church of England, in so far as it too began to give theological sanction to divorce. Thus it is proper to say that the introduction of facilities for divorce is something that has historically developed together with secularization.

One may well ask what all this has to do with politics and the question of the duty of State in the matter of divorce. The answer is simple and short. It is that the State has a political obligation to resist the secularization of a Christian society. The reason for this—as has been ably pointed out recently by Father Danielou in his book *Prayer as a Political Problem* (London, 1967)—is that

176

there is a spiritual dimension to the common good, which urges that the State should do what it can to secure the well-being of the politico-social framework, within which its citizens are enabled to live their religious and moral lives. For such a framework is virtually necessary to underpin the personal persuasions of men in the mass. It provides support to conformism—a support of which the average man stands in need. Have not sociological surveys of lapsing from their religion by Irish and other groups in Britain made it clear that this is due, not so much to a weak faith or a poor education in their religion, but rather to the effect of a psycho-sociological uprooting which deprives them of the social helps to religious practice? The fish out of water cannot breathe, much though he strives to do so.

Thus it is with the religion and morals of the ordinary man—the average man in the street. It is not that their religion and morals is spurious but rather that it is their kind of religion and morals, with its own relative value and validity. Not for them is the purer religion and morality of the *élite*—with its bare altars, abstract art, formal hymns and self-imposed poverty. That such must remain the posture of an intellectual minority is the lesson of human history and original sin. By all means one should work towards better things, but to think that a strong, upstanding, entirely personal religious and moral practice can be achieved short of a long-distance Teilhardian future, would be as unrealistic as to believe that the mass of the people can be made to appreciate the art of a Picasso or a Braque rather than the intimate humanism of a Teniers or an Ostade. It is for this reason that, despite the strictures of Richard Egenter in his book *The Desecration of Christ* (London, 1967), the holy pictures of traditional vintage that we know so well—the innocent Madonnas of the ordination cards and the Sacred Hearts of the Irish firesides—represent a religious epoch than in which, as somebody has remarked, "Christ never had a better innings".

It is for such reasons also—if one may digress for a moment—that the Irish Bishops were rather preoccupied during the Vatican Council with safeguarding the needs of mass religion. People like Daphne Pochin-Mould were able to point to shortcomings on their part in matters liturgical, due to what was thought to be an inadequate appreciation of the importance of "participation". The problem of the Irish Bishops was, on the one hand, the large scale church-going population and, on the other, that greatest participation is to be had in more personal circumstances, as in small churches. This kind of thing often creates a difficult dilemma, which cannot be escaped from without sacrificing something. Surely it is its emphasis on the importance of communal participation in the Church at every level that puts the New Left Church in Britain in the anomalous position of being a sort of Socialist Church that is not a Church of the masses. For large-scale practice of necessity entails a degree of non-communal or institutionalized religion which is entirely abhorrent to the New Left.

What I am really getting at is the need for a patterned sociological framework which will give support to the religious and moral beliefs of the average man and thus help him to live his life in accordance with them. What he needs, if you will, is a prop to his weakness, but then this is the purpose of all society in all domains. Political society or the State is no exception. Its legal system represents a fabric of social values that are intended to sustain the individual through social living. This is the function of a constitutional provision which prohibits divorce in a society composed predominantly of people who believe it wrong to practise it.

For the legislature to take account of this community attitude is by no means to enforce morality by means of law. This is something that is frequently misunderstood. During a visit to Canada a couple of years ago I found the new Prime Minister—Pierre Elliott Trudeau, a Catholic—agreeing to new legislation which would liberalize the laws of divorce, on the grounds that it was not at all his function as statesman to "legislate for sin". And this of course is entirely true. But it is not, by a long chalk, to "legislate for sin" to recognize that there is a spiritual dimension to the common good and to seek as statesman to do nothing that would injure the framework of social living which assists the mass of the people to work out their salvation. On the contrary to fail to do so is bad politics. It is to weaken, if not destroy, the infra-structure of morality which the generality of people need so badly. And it is to do so under the guise of a tolerance which would force the majority of the people to accept the social values of the minority.

Undoubtedly where a situation of genuine pluralism exists—as is the case in Canada taken as a whole—good politics decrees a more open system of social values. For this reason Prime Minister Trudeau's stance in the matter of divorce is quite justified, even if the principle which he enunciated stands in need of qualification. And in point of fact the Canadian Bishops have not opposed his measure in practice. Ireland, on the other hand, is not Canada. I know that there have been people—among them priests—who have been quick to designate our society "pluralist". I have to ask myself, however, what exactly is meant? On a particular issue in which the voice of the minority is particularly small, is one entitled to accede to it in the name of pluralism? Where indeed is one to draw the line? Does pluralism in fact obtain, as Jacques Maritain once said, where even one voice strikes a note of dissent? If so there never was but a pluralist society. Given this approach one should abandon the criterion of social values when considering legislation and should substitute for it a kind of sociological empiricism or counting of heads, with a view to accommodating everybody and permitting everything. Some societies are endeavouring to do just this. The resulting "secular city" is so injurious to man that I am surprised to find that Maritain—who in other books went to such pains to disestablish what he called in contrast the "sacred city" of our forefathers—should, in his book *The Peasant of the Garonne* (London, 1967), bemoan the fruit of the contemporary liberal trend in matters ecclesial yet have no regrets about the same thing in the political domain.

In a society in which pluralism is not accentuated, the political ideal would seem to be the construction of a legal system which will maintain the fabric of the social values of the people as a whole while allowing the genuine rights of all minorities. This creates inevitable problems, which are far from easy to solve in the concrete. It is sometimes hard to know what genuine rights really are, and sometimes impossible to reconcile the conflicting rights of sections of the people.

Even rights of conscience are sometimes hard to recognize and even harder to reconcile with social values. Take, for example, the question of whether a religion based on drug-taking should be allowed to exist in contemporary American society. Art Cleps, self-styled Boo Hoo of The Neo-American Church, Millbrook, New York has expounded the position of his followers. He writes:

> As I have wearily explained to at least a dozen curious cops, knowing full well that I might as well be addressing the nearest wall in Chinese, the practice of our religion is as dear to us as life itself. And we cannot practise our religion without the sacraments of our religion, which are the psychedelic

substances. You would think that an Irish Catholic policeman would grasp this simple concept at once, since it resembles so closely concepts upon which his own basic loyalties and motivations are presumably organised. Not so. It is a notion that seems to him as alien as moon dust. I fear this is not a religious or materialistic society. It is a zombi society, and that is what we are trying to change.

As far as contemporary Ireland is concerned, once it is clear that divorce and secularization have gone together historically, it is equally clear that politicians, qua politicians, have a very grave duty to exercise care if by introducing divorce legislation they would find themselves "rocking the boat" in the direction of secularism. If Irish society should ever go that way of its own accord, its politicians will undoubtedly recognize the trend and have a right and duty, qua politicians, to deal with it. In other words, a time may come when the clear majority of the population will positively call for the introduction of divorce. Can today's politician say that this time has already come? If not, why should he stimulate its coming? Would it not be time enough to cater for it when once arrived? Indeed should not the wisdom of the politician be employed in seeking ways and means—in so far as lies within his province—of staving off that day as long as possible?

The fact that other countries have gone that way is no argument. Things are not necessarily right just because people tend to do them. If this were so, then the contemporary trend towards uncontrolled urbanism, monster universities, or the proliferation of nuclear armaments would also be right and proper. Yet nobody would suggest for a moment that it would not be a better thing if the nuclear club could be disbanded. And the day is not far off—I am genuinely convinced—when there will be a reaction against the inhumanity of megalopolis and against the pursuit of learning in the setting of universities that have grown too big. May we not also hope for a reaction against the secularist trend that has led Western Christian civilization to the brink of disintegration? The truth is that there is a real need for a revival of social values if the West is not to go down before a non-Western world that, for all its faults, stands for some basic values of its own. In this revival, once again as it did in the past, should not Ireland strive to be a light in the darkness? Let us not forget our sense of history.

One has to admit, I agree, that any progressive society has to afford due place to elements of change as well as to those of conservation. That diehard traditionalism is bad for society, and that there is need for a liberal stimulus to counter it, is a sound general political principle. But it should be related to society as found in the concrete. Thus the contribution of the liberal stimulus is unquestionably valuable in the context of a backward looking, quite closed, conservative society. At the other extreme, in that of a wholly liberal, permissive society, there is need rather for the fostering of a sound conservatism. Today in our mixed—partly conservative and partly liberal—Irish society, it seems to me that one should be unusually careful about introducing a liberal stimulus in the direction of secularization. Where has this led Britain even in our own time—from a proud empire to a giggling society?

The pace of change is fast enough without forcing it. Ireland today—with its anti-establishment magazines, its non-conformist associations and its over-influential outsider-type personalities and programmes, has a numerous enough band of representatives of the liberal stimulus. One has to ask, therefore, whether there is need or

reason for its politicians to jump on the band-wagon—
thereby hastening the day when this Ireland of ours
could be as different from the Irish and Catholic society
that we know as secularism is from Christianity. At
bottom, the choice is one for the politician himself. It is
a question not only of the rights of the consciences of
others but of the duties of his own individual conscience.
Quite obviously his responsibility is unenviable.

As far as divorce goes, legal people as well as moralists
have to agree that if its introduction were to run
counter to the public welfare, which is only another way
of saying the interests of the people as a whole, it would
not be sound legislation in the highest sense of that
word. As Senator John Kelly has put it: "If we considered that objective social reasons, independent of our
Catholic beliefs as individuals, weighed more heavily
against divorce than in favour of it, then I think we are
entitled to keep our law as it is and need not apologize
for doing so" (*The Sunday Press,* 7 March, 1971).

But to return to contraception and abortion as well
as divorce. On 11 March, 1971, following their meeting
at Maynooth, the Irish Hierarchy declared that they
fully shared "the disquiet, which is widespread among
the people at the present time, regarding pressures being
exerted on public opinion on questions concerning the
civil law on divorce, contraception and abortion".
They went on:

> These questions involve issues of grave import
> for society as a whole, which go far beyond purely
> private morality or private religious belief. Civil
> law on these matters should respect the wishes of
> the people who elected the legislators and the
> bishops confidently hope that the legislators them-
> selves will respect this important principle (*The Irish
> Times,* 12 March, 1971).

In other words, as Cardinal Conway explained, the question reduces itself to a matter concerned with the public good, with the kind of society that is wanted. It is not a question of merely private morality.

The reaction of some to this *prise de position* was to complain that genuine fears for the passing of a way of life in Ireland, and its replacement by the permissive society, are no justification for a closing of the door by the legislature on matters which an adult people felt entitled to decide for themselves.

This argument is more specious than convincing. In point of fact it rests, either on the attribution of an unqualified right on the part of a minority or minorities to override majority interests in certain areas relating to conduct which are regarded as purely private, or else, on the attribution to the majority of an unqualified right to introduce what legislation they wish in such areas.

Neither attribution is correct. As far as the form of the argument goes, one must simply "deny the major". By this I mean that it is difficult, if not impossible, to maintain a sharp distinction between those areas of personal conduct (call them moral if you wish), which clearly fall within the competence of the State and those others which lie outside this. That there is room for endless debate on where the dividing line lies, history bears eloquent witness. But about the principle involved there can be no doubt: a great deal of what is regarded rightly as pertaining to the domain of private morality pertains also to that of public. It is for this reason that "immoral" acts like murder or rape or robbery are also "criminal" acts.

As far as the second attribution goes, while it is indeed an important principle that legislators should respect the wishes of the people who elected them, this must always be on the assumption that what the people wish is itself acceptable morally. Not that the law should ever be concerned with enforcing the moral teaching of any church as regards what is moral in the realm of private behaviour. Rather is it the position that the consciences of the legislators may be compelled to baulk if faced by a demand— even from the people as a whole—for the introduction of a measure which is so abhorrent to the moral persuasions of the legislators themselves that to allow it to be incorporated into the legal structure of the State would, in their minds, be to subvert public morality.

Democracy is far from being either omniscient or infallible, ambition omnicompetence though it may. The people most certainly can sometimes do wrong and it is up to their representatives to endeavour to ensure otherwise. Is it not for this reason, among others, that Rousseau's original "cab-driver" theory of democracy (implying that the elected representatives of the people are entirely in the hands of their constituents, whose directives they should passively obey) had to be replaced. The alternative theory is that of "free representation", according to which the people's representatives decide for themselves what best serves their people—taking account not only of the "felt needs" of their local electorate but of the wider interests of the national community as a whole and of the limitations imposed on legislators by the moral law. To deny this would be to opt for totalitarian democracy, legal positivism, political absolutism—the lot. How ironical that an argument which is intended to expound a liberal vindication of the private rights of the individual should end up at the very opposite end of the scale! But then it would not be the first time that a doctrinaire approach such as this should find itself suddenly involved in an alliance at the practical level with an inverse state of affairs. Hoisted with its own petard!

Recognizing this danger, the Wolfenden Report in Britain—to which Dr. O'Callaghan, Professor of Moral

Theology at Maynooth has drawn attention—was quite
definite that:

> The function of the criminal law is to preserve
> public order and decency, to protect the citizen from
> what is offensive and injurious, and to provide
> sufficient safeguard against exploitation and cor-
> ruption of others, particularly those who are specific-
> ally vulnerable because they are young, weak in
> body or mind, inexperienced . . . . .

It is true that in many countries legislation in accordance with this political philosophy exists which excludes
certain forms of behaviour by reason of the fact that,
when it was first introduced, the religious and moral
attitudes of the people were such that the behaviour
in question was generally accepted as not only privately
but publicly immoral. It is true too that in matters such
as this, the attitude of the community can change. But
before plunging ahead with dismantling legislation of this
kind, the representatives of the people should be satisfied
that they have respected the twin obligations which
burden them (a) of ensuring that the people really want
such change and (b) that the people are right in wanting it.

12

On Balancing Innovation and Conservation

IN A PREVIOUS chapter I have emphasized the need to strike a balance in society between its equally essential institutional and community aspects. On reflection it will be realized that this was also to emphasize the need for room in society for the forces of innovation and conservation.

Unless there be room in society for the emergence and containing of the kind of people who make for change, that society is doomed to stagnation. No progress is possible without some change; which in turn depends on the presence of people who initiate change —if necessary by protest and revolution. On the other hand, unless a balance is maintained by correlative forces of conservation, society will become rudderless and adrift; an anarchical chaos is inevitable.

It is interesting to note in how many different ways sociologists and social psychologists have been saying this. The very founder of social psychology himself— Gabriel Tarde (1843–1904)—went so far as to describe social interaction as a whole in terms simply of innova-

tion and conservation. The former he termed invention,
the latter imitation. In fact, he defined society as a col-
lection of people inventing and imitating continuously.

It should be noted that Tarde made a rigid distinction
between what he called "imitation-tradition" and "imita-
tion-fashion". Imitation tradition tends to reproduce a
behaviour model after the exact manner of previous
generations, imitation fashion along the lines practised
by contemporaries. Within each there is both positive and
negative imitation, viz. the reproduction of a model or
its opposite, which latter, in an inverted but real sense,
is truly a species of imitation.

Society, said Tarde, is like a lake. Ripples on it are
set up by the forces of invention, some of which wave-
lets coincide, while others contend with one another.
He was but saying that society subsists on innovation and
conservation.

More recently, David Riesman, author of *The Lonely
Crowd*, has spoken of essentially the same thing under
still different terminology. Members of society, as he
sees them, fall into three categories. Firstly, there is
the type which he calls "inner-directed"—the non-conformist, the outsider, the innovator—whose line of action
is determined by nothing if not his conscience. Secondly
and thirdly, there are the "tradition-directed" and the
"other-directed" types. These are the people who follow
respectively the ways of their ancestors or the habits
of the folk next door. Both of them must be classed
as conservators, thus bringing us back again to the
basic twin forces of innovation and conservation in
society.

The fact should not be missed, however, that Riesman
sees conservation as itself falling into two distinct kinds.
In this, one is reminded of Tarde's division of imitation.
Of course there is at the same time a world of difference
between tradition-direction and other-direction. The

former stems from an appreciation of what has gone before, the latter of what one's peers are doing. Either, of course, can be praiseworthy and either can be open to reproof. If a slavish effort to keep up with what is being done round about one can indeed be reprehensible, so also can a blind belief in the value of traditions if it makes for a total lack of receptivity to new ideas. Indeed, tradition-direction and other-direction in themselves and without some counterbalancing by inner-direction, are insufficient to meet the needs of society.

And so you have the see-saw. Whether one speaks of invention and imitation, liberalism and traditionalism, innovation and conservation, does not really matter. What does matter is that in every stable and yet dynamic society each of these poles must be represented. And while it would be far too facile to identify these dualities too closely with that of conscience and law, there is a point up to which there is a meeting between them.

Each of the poles in question has to be balanced against the other if due order with due progress is to be achieved. We can see this clearly in the case of conservation which, unless ample allowance is made for some progressivism, is nothing but a backward-looking obscurantism. In the case of the Church, Vatican II provided plenty of examples of conservatives of both these kinds, the liberalist and the traditionalist groups.

Innovation has exactly analogous problems. For if it is to be effective and to accomplish what it sets out to do in society, it has perforce to accept the basic social framework. If it is so extreme as to neglect this or to come into direct confrontation with it, the chances are that it will not be successful. Not, at least, without re-sorting to the violence which has been historically as-sociated with rebellion, because otherwise the innovation and its sponsors are likely to be snuffed out by the backlash of the establishment whose societal foundations are threatened. This indeed is the stuff out of which past revolutions have been made and the rock on which innovation has often foundered.

It is seldom enough that innovation which formally represents a system of things that is incompatible with the texture of existing society, has managed to survive and overcome without violence. The failure of so many Socialist movements of the nineteenth century, of the more extreme university restructuring efforts of the twentieth century and of scores of other examples of the same kind of thing, is sufficient proof of the validity of the point. And yet there are also examples from history which show that there are exceptions to the rule. The eventual success of Christianity is one of them.

This very example should be sufficient to illustrate the difficult judgement that has to be made by social authority when deciding how much and what kind of innovation it is prepared to allow in the society which it governs. Without some innovation, there will be stagnation. With too much of it, the society may be overthrown. It is a salutary thought to remember that in their day and age and in the context of their society, the Apostles bearing the symbol of their crucified Master must have seemed not unlike a small group of Maoists today waving the little red book of their Chairman.

If this kind of thing is inevitable, as indeed it normally is, it behoves innovators whose contestation of their society runs really deep, to seek ways and means of attaining their end without being repressed. It is for this reason that reformist movements have always a greater chance of success—provided they really do keep up pressure for what they stand for—than extreme liberal revolutionary movements. Or rather, what is quite certain is that they can be successful without resorting to violence, in a way that the latter cannot.

And yet, as is also well known, the reformist approach

has never been acceptable to the more animated innovators of the past—from the Young Ireland rebels versus the O'Connellites in Irish history, to Roger Garaudy (expelled from the French Communist Party in 1970 for moderate policies) versus Fidel Castro or Che Guevara. Indeed the majority of contemporary Communist youth—whether claiming to be Marxist or Maoist in inspiration—have but little time for reformist innovation.

It should not be forgotten that, despite its emphasis on the thesis that Capitalist society will yield place to Socialist only by way of revolution, official Marxism—or at any rate the Marxism of Marx himself—has always allowed room for the accomplishment of the revolution by means other than violent rebellion.

At the Congress of the Socialist International at Amsterdam in 1872 Marx himself made the following important remark:

> We do not assert that the way to reach this goal (i.e. Communism) is the same everywhere. We know that the institutions, manners, and the customs of the various countries must be considered and we do not deny that there are countries like England and America, and, if I understand your arrangements better, I might even add Holland, where the worker may attain his object by peaceful means. But not in all countries is this the case. (Quoted by Kautsky in *The Dictatorship of the Proletariat*, p. 10.)

A first-class example of how this can be effected has been provided in Chile by the accession to power of President Allende and his revolutionary government through the constitutional use of the machinery of democracy. In an important interview between Allende and Régis Debray (author of *Revolution in the Revolu-*

tion) published in *The Sunday Times* (14 March, 1971) we get a useful insight into some points worth recording here.

Debray: What is the lesson for Latin America to be drawn from what is happening in Chile?

Allende: The lesson is that each country has its own particular circumstances, and we must act according to these circumstances. There is no set formula. We have arrived through the polling booths. Apparently it can be said we are mere reformists, but we have done things which show that we mean to make the revolution.

Debray: You know how in the overall picture of Latin America your image is contrasted with those of Fidel and Che. What do you think of those who say that what has just happened in Chile gives the lie to the thesis of the people's war, to the validity of the armed struggle elsewhere?

Allende: The revolutionary struggle may be found in the guerilla camp or in urban insurrection; or it may be insurrection through the polling booths; it depends on the content it is given.

The Christian Church—itself a revolutionary movement in a very real sense—has a somewhat similar problem as that of Marxism in respect of the place of reform as against revolution as a means of accomplishing its purpose. For despite its own revolutionary origins, the Church can scarcely be said to be disposed towards accepting revolution in the pursuit of its objectives in either secular or religious society. Was not this very point one of the main issues at stake in the debate between Fathers Metz and Baum at the Brussels meeting of theologians in 1970?

Officially in fact, the Church does not accept revolution as a normal means of effecting even desirable change. In particular, revolution by way of the use of physical force has always been regarded as a last resort. While at the theoretical level a grudging assent is given to the use of force in certain circumstances, not only has the use of it been hedged round by strict conditions, but in practice it has seldom been clearly favoured. The value of retaining the *status quo* as against introducing disorder has always been pointed out.

As far as the internal life of the Church itself is concerned, revolution is certainly not acceptable. Whoever therefore sets before himself the bringing about of revolutionary change in any particular aspect of the life of the Church, has to seek it by way of reformist methods. This may cause the impatient to grow weary or lash out; the prudent will know how to use it to advantage.

To conclude: it is much too easy to declare that revolutionary changes are needed before old and established institutions are rendered acceptable. One gets glimpses of how this temptation can take hold of men in books such as Charles Davis's *A Question of Conscience* (London, 1967) and James Kavanagh's *A Modern Priest Looks at his Outdated Church* (New York, 1967). It is very much more difficult to live with a problem, to seek to deal with it within the circumstantial limitations in which one finds oneself—in short, it is more difficult to flee revolt and work positively towards reform. And yet gradual reform can, in its own way, eventually effect revolutionary change.

241
New   7930
AUTHOR
Newman, Jeremiah
TITLE
Conscience Versus Law
DATE | ROOM

241
New   7930